The Oil of Joy

The Oil of Joy

FOR MOURNING

365 daily meditations to comfort the widowed

DR. JAN SHEBLE

HENDRICKSON
PUBLISHERS

The Oil of Joy for Mourning
Copyright © 1997 by Hendrickson Publishers, Inc.
P.O. Box 3473
Peabody, Massachusetts 01961-3473

Printed in the United States of America

ISBN 1-56563-303-2

First printing—October 1997

Unless otherwise noted, all Scripture references in this book are taken from the Holy Bible: New International Version, copyright 1973, 1978, 1984 by the International Bible Society.

Cover design by Paetzold Design, Batavia, Ill.
Interior by Pinpoint Marketing, Kirkland, Wash.
Edited by Judy Bodmer and Heather Stroobosscher

Library of Congress Cataloging-in-Publication Data

Sheble, Jan, 1931–
    The oil of joy for mourning: 365 daily meditations to comfort the widowed / Jan Sheble
        p.   cm.
    ISBN 1-56563-303-2 (cloth)
    1. Widows—Prayer books and devotions—English. 2. Widowers—Prayer books and devotions—English.   3. Devotional calendars.
I. Title.
BV4528.S48   1997   97-28489
242' .4—dc21   CIP

Dedication

To my husband, Earl, who now resides in the presence of our Lord and Savior, Jesus Christ.

Acknowledgements

I thank the Lord for all the experiences of my life.

I also am grateful to:

Dan Penwell of Hendrickson Publishers for his confidence in me.

Judy Bodmer, Heather Stroobosscher, and Scott Pinzon for sharing their editorial expertise.

My sisters of the Brandon Day chapter of Aglow International for their encouragement.

My daughter and son-in-law, Ron and Sue Hymer for their concrete assistance.

Preface

To give unto them beauty for ashes, the oil of joy for mourning, the garment of praise for the spirit of heaviness; that they might be called trees of righteousness, the planting of the LORD* that he might be glorified. (Isaiah 61:3 KJV)

During our trek through this earthly life, we encounter many losses. One of the deepest of these is when death takes a husband or a wife from us. Although we may have kindred feeling with others who have lost their spouses, we each grieve in our own way. There is one who knows each of us, understands us completely, and shares our deepest sorrow. That one is the Lord Jesus Christ.

He speaks to us through his love letter, the Bible. With these words from Isaiah, he specifically offers consolation. You'll find the thread of this verse, as written in the King James Version (KJV), throughout this book. Accept what our God has to say. Crawl up into his lap and let him be your Abba Father.

---

* In the NIV Old Testament, the word LORD appears in small capital letters. This is the English version of the Hebrew personal and covenant name of God, YHWH (Yahweh.) In the NIV New Testament, the word Lord appears with upper and lower case letters. Our Lord Jesus Christ has fulfilled the role of our Redeemer and covenant Lord.

The meditations in this book have mostly been inspired by the words of the Scriptures as written in the New International Version (NIV). You will find a meditation written for each day of the calendar year. It is my belief that the discipline of a daily devotional can be helpful during times of stress in our lives.

So, dear child of God, try to get yourself into the habit of reading this devotional each day. On each page, you'll find a prayer focus. You will see that the suggested prayer for each day addresses issues not necessarily related to grieving, It is when we look beyond our own pain that we can begin the process of healing of our deepest sorrow. Please include these topics in your daily prayers. Others who are also using this devotional are praying along with you. What power is possible in the corporate prayers of believers!

If, at the end of one year of using this devotional, you find you need to start over again, that's all right. You need time to adjust to your new pattern of life. Be gentle with yourself. Be patient. Let the love of God overflow and cover you with his oil of joy for your mourning.

In Christ,
Jan Sheble

JANUARY 1

Beauty for ashes. (Isaiah 61:3 KJV)

Have you ever seen a field fire? The flames rage and burn with such intensity that no one can come near. After the fire is finally over, what's left? Ashes, my dear child of God.

Sound like what you've been through in your loss? The heart of your grief flared up around and engulfed you, and there was nothing you could do about it. What was left is what you live with now: dark, sooty ashes.

But wait, look what happens in the aftermath of a burned field. It may seem there's nothing left, no hope of renewal, but gently, surely, new green growth appears from the charred roots and the parched ground. There is new life. Beauty begins to appear once again.

Maybe, dear one, the fire you have been through was really a "controlled burn." Maybe it was not raging indiscriminately, but was allowed to happen by a Father God who is well able to be in charge. Trust him and let him show you how he plans to give you beauty for ashes.

Prayer focus for today: Those who need to forget what went before.

JANUARY 2

> *You are a shield around me, O LORD; you bestow glory
> on me and lift up my head.* (Psalm 3:3)

Why do I need a shield? That was only for the days of knights in shining armor, right? Wrong!

We all need shields because there are darts being sent our way daily by the Enemy. These darts bear names such as Doubt, Insecurity, and Being Misunderstood. Our defense is the perfect protection offered by our Lord Jesus Christ.

If we're truly wise, we'll crouch down, figuratively, and let the shield of Jesus fend off these attacks. When we do this, we can look up and see the pure light, the glory of his perfect love for us.

So, dear child of God, don't be embarrassed to hide behind his shield of faith. He promises to bestow glory on you and lift you up!

Prayer focus for today: Those who feel no one cares about them.

"Man does not live on bread alone, but on every word that comes from the mouth of God." (Matthew 4:4)

B read? Who can eat at a time like this? Maybe you felt that way at first, and maybe you still do. But think about why the Lord provides us with our daily bread.

He made us and knows what we need to sustain ourselves. Therefore he provides us food. It is a disservice to him not to care for the body he has chosen to house your soul. Part of that caring is eating balanced meals.

But that's not all we need. Jesus reminds us that we live on the word that comes from the mouth of God. He made us and knows what our souls need to be sustained, a balanced diet of his Holy Word.

So, especially at this time, begin to take care of your body and your soul by ingesting all that he has provided for you.

Prayer focus for today: Prison chaplains.

JANUARY 4

"The LORD is my rock, my fortress and my deliverer;
my God is my rock, in whom I take refuge."
(2 Samuel 22:2–3)

Our God is so good to us! He gives us word pictures to describe himself. He does this because he really wants us to understand his care for us.

So, he tells us he is a rock. What does a rock make you think of? Do you see it as something solid and indestructible? Man may feebly try to move it or change its shape, but rock remains strong.

Think of rock shoals, for instance, that have been cut back for major road building. Those vertical lines you see are evidence of the holes drilled for the blasting of the rocks with dynamite. And did all that explosive power destroy the rock? No, only a tiny slice of it was removed.

So, relax and know that you can depend on the truth that the Lord is a mighty rock.

Prayer focus for today: Christian authors.

JANUARY 5

*Is anything too hard for the L*ORD*?* (Genesis 18:14)

The three-year-old crawled up to a top shelf and brought down a three hundred-piece jigsaw puzzle. With great glee, he opened the box and poured all the pieces onto the table.

He tried to fit one piece to another. But he soon realized that there was no way he could put all those pieces together. He sobbed, "It's too hard!"

Maybe you feel a little like that three-year-old. Your life has been shattered into at least a million pieces. You can't make sense of what's happened. It's just too hard! You feel like sobbing.

Well, sob if you must. That's OK. But look at what the Lord promises in his question, "Is anything too hard for me?"

He means that. Nothing is too hard for him. He can take all those million pieces and pull them all together to make your life beautiful and complete. Only trust him!

Prayer focus for today: Traveling business persons who are lonely.

JANUARY 6

You have been a refuge for the poor, a refuge for the needy in his distress. (Isaiah 25:4)

Been out in a rainstorm lately? You're walking down the street and the sky begins to fall. Your car is blocks away. Meanwhile, you're getting wetter and wetter.

And then you look ahead. There's an alcove in a building. You scurry into it where it's dry. You have reached a *refuge*.

A refuge can be defined as a shelter or protection from danger and distress. Maybe the rainstorm doesn't really threaten you with *danger,* but getting soaked can cause *distress.* Isn't that a little like your life right now? Cares and concerns come pelting down upon you, and they surely give rise to distress.

Where is your refuge? Well, the Lord tells us in this verse that he already is and has always been your refuge. It's been done. The respite from the torrent has been provided. All we have to do is accept his protection.

Praise be the God of refuge!

Prayer focus for today: A cure for muscular dystrophy and for those affliced with it.

The LORD your God will bless you in the land you are entering to possess. (Deuteronomy 30:16)

Try to imagine what it was like to be one of the children of Israel wandering around the barren land for years. Were they "happy campers"? Hardly!

They whined. They complained. They even wished to go back to Egypt but knew they couldn't really do that. When they focused on *where they were* at the moment and *where they had been,* they were miserable.

They forgot why they were called out of Egypt so they could possess the new land the Lord had promised them.

Before we're too critical of the children of Israel, we need to look at ourselves in our momentary situation. We may wish we could return to Egypt, to what *was,* knowing that's not possible. We can be miserable about where we are today, or we can make the best of this time of wandering through the barren land of our life.

We then will be ready to enter the new land the Lord has promised. This "new land" is the new life he has planned for us.

Trust in the Father God who knows what is best.

Prayer focus for today: Refugees.

JANUARY 8

"But whoever lives by the truth comes into the light."
(John 3:21)

Lord, I've known you a long time. I've studied your word and I've tried to do what you want me to do. I've done my best. I've lived by your truth.

Why have put me into the murky darkness of bereavement? Why can't I see the light while I'm in this tunnel of grief? Where is your truth in all this?

And then your voice comes to me: "My dear, precious child, the truth is the gospel. The truth is my Son, Jesus Christ. Trust in him alone."

When I trust in him only, I will see the light, for he alone is the Light.

Thank you, Lord, for pointing this out to me. It's true, I've known you for a long time. Now I need to rest on that firm foundation of knowing you and look upward to receive a measure of your truth and your light.

Prayer focus for today: Teachers' aides.

"But I will gain glory for myself through Pharaoh and all his army, and the Egyptians will know that I am the Lord.*"* (Exodus 14:4)

Do you remember back to your school days? Think about being on the playground. Was it always a happy time? Or were there times when you were terrorized by the school bully?

Pharaoh was a little like the school bully. Perhaps he was the terror of the playground at Cairo Middle School. And what was worse, he had a whole army who did what he told them to do.

Why did God choose to use Pharaoh to demonstrate the power of the Lord? He's the *Lord,* that's why! Sometimes he chooses the most unlikely situations or persons so we can really see his power.

Why did the Lord choose to put you in your situation now? This bereavement stuff can strike terror in your heart. Why, Lord?

Because, dear child of God, he can really show his power in unlikely situations. He alone knows the good that will result from this.

And when we look back on this, we will see in a fuller way that he is Lord!

Prayer focus for today: Students in inner city schools.

JANUARY 10

"You will grieve, but your grief will turn to joy."
(John 16:20)

You must have heard the expression, "I never promised you a rose garden." OK, but I'll bet you never signed up for this bunch of thorns better known as grief.

The Lord has told us we will grieve. Why do you suppose he allows this?

Maybe he allows us to wallow in the bramble bush of the thorns of grief so we can appreciate the sweet aroma of the roses when grief turns to joy.

That's one of the greatest things about our God. He may allow unpleasant things to enter our lives and bereavement to touch us, but he causes us to rise above this by turning it all around for good. What joy that instills in us!

Praise him for the joy that he promised will come!

Prayer focus for today: Christians who strive to learn more of the Lord.

The salvation of the righteous comes from the LORD; he is their stronghold in time of trouble. (Psalm 37:39)

You know how it is when you're driving down an interstate highway. The traffic seems to go faster and faster. Before you know it, you're right in the middle of a pack of over-speeding vehicles. Cars to the right of you and cars to the left of you are going way over the posted speed limit. You begin to feel uncomfortable because you don't see a way out of this racing frenzy.

And then ahead, off to the right, there is a white car with red and blue flashing lights on the roof. It's a police officer who has pulled over a driver.

What happens? The traffic immediately slows and you begin to feel a little safer. The mere presence of that officer calmed your situation.

It's a little bit like what the Lord does for us. He promises us that he will be our salvation and our protection. Just as the police officer causes the rushing traffic to slow down and keep you safe, so the Lord by his persevering presence protects and guards you.

Prayer focus for today: Those who volunteer at soup kitchens.

JANUARY 12

All my longings lie open before you, O Lord; my sighing is not hid from you. (Psalm 38:9)

Ever since I lost my spouse, I am reminded that I "sigh" a lot. I'm not even conscious of it, but those around me say, "You're doing it again!"

And I long, how I long, for what might have been. Those plans, hopes, dreams my spouse and I had for the future are gone, but I do long for the impossible.

Does the Lord see this? Does he hear my sighs? Indeed he does. Nothing is hidden from his eyes. Nothing is hidden from his heart.

When I sigh, he sighs with me. Any longings I have, he understands with his perfection. I need to be willing to rest in the truth that he alone truly sees all and still loves me.

Prayer focus for today: Governors and other state officials.

"I will praise you forever for what you have done; in your name I will hope, for your name is good." (Psalm 52:9)

You may have heard that today is the yesterday of tomorrow. It's just another of those expressions that demonstrate how obsessed we are with time. We measure our days, hours, and minutes, think about yesterday, and plan for tomorrow. It seems as if we're trying to blot out today.

In the final analysis, all our measurement of time doesn't mean a thing. It's merely our human way to try to make sense of our days.

The Lord knows this and is gentle with us. The important thing we need to remember is what he has done for us. He has assured us of our salvation by the Blood of the Lamb.

In response to this, our joy is to know we will praise him forever. If today is painful for us because of our loss, remember what he has done and that we will be with him forever.

It does tend to put today in the right perspective.

Prayer focus for today: Parents who have children in day care.

JANUARY 14

Set your hearts on things above, where Christ is seated at the right hand of God. (Colossians 3:1)

Someone once said, "If you can keep your head when others around you are losing theirs, perhaps you don't understand the situation!"

The world may look at you now and remind you of that saying. They may wonder how you cope with your bereavement. They may even suggest that you're not facing reality.

But when you know Jesus, you can set your heart on things above. You can keep your head even when the situation seems impossible to understand.

Even if setting your heart on things above seems difficult while you're in the pangs of bereavement, try to do it anyway! Focus on Jesus Christ. Think of where he is seated, at the right hand of God!

Prayer focus for today: Those who are spiritually blind.

Be on your guard; stand firm in the faith.
(1 Corinthians 16:13)

One of the cardinal rules when playing team sports is "keep your eye on the ball." Loosely translated, this means stay alert and be on your guard. Even those of us who are klutzes can understand this.

This is sound advice for us in other circumstances as well. At times in our lives, we need to keep our eye on the ball no matter what threatens to get in the way.

If the myriad of details relating to the legal issues surrounding the death of your spouse threaten to get you down, keep your eye on the ball.

If enticing-but-wrong relationships seem appealing to you at this vulnerable time, be on your guard.

If worry about the future comes thundering over you, keep your eye on the ball. Stand firm and watch how your faith will pull you through.

Prayer focus for today: Spouses who are unequally yoked.

JANUARY 16

Praise be to the Lord, to God our Savior, who daily bears our burdens. (Psalm 68:19)

We live in a time of shared responsibilities. We have Mr. Moms changing diapers and women driving semi-trucks. Advocates of equal employment insist that ninety-eight-pound females can hoist cargo as well as 250-pound Atlases.

There's nothing inherently wrong with men and women being treated equally. But somewhere in the shuffle of all this, maybe we are taking on too many burdens.

Now at this time of adjustment in your life, do you feel the burdens are too many or too heavy?

Are you bogged down under them?

Look at this verse from the psalmist. He tells us that the Lord God daily bears our burdens. We have his perfect promise that he's there for us—all the time. He also assures us that our burdens are his. He willingly takes them on.

Give up or at least share your burdens with him who consistently, daily bears them for you.

Prayer focus for today: Workers in fast food establishments.

If anyone is in Christ, he is a new creation.
(2 Corinthians 5:17)

Advertisers tell us their products will revolutionize our lives. "Use this shampoo." "Join our health club." "Our diet system will create a 'new you'."

Can you believe these claims? Can anyone really be made new by using cosmetics or diet plans?

Of course, the answer is no. But there is one way to be a new creation. That way is to be in Christ, to walk with him, and to seek his face daily.

When you are made new by being in Christ, you are not bogged down with the past. You are truly new. He wants you to get a new attitude.

What can that mean to you at this time of your life? How can you feel like a new creation in the midst of your loss?

Dear child of God, be *in* Christ. He promised to make you new, and he never forgets his promises.

Prayer focus for today: Bible colleges.

JANUARY 18

We give thanks to you, O God, we give thanks, for your Name is near; men tell of your wonderful deeds. You say, "I choose the appointed time." (Psalm 75:1–2)

L ord, you tell us in your word that you choose the appointed time. That means you chose the exact moment and time for my spouse to die. No matter what circumstances, it was your time. You chose it. Neither human discoveries nor medical or mechanical devices could alter what you chose.

I know I should just accept this. I do, most of the time. But, Lord, child as I am, sometimes I ask, "Why? Why so soon? Why now?"

Then your answer comes to me: "Look at all the words of these verses. Give thanks to me, the Lord, for wonderful deeds."

Does this mean that the appointed time was one of your "wonderful" deeds? In the scheme of eternity, I can only answer, "Yes, Lord. Not my will, but yours."

I will thank you forever.

Prayer focus for today: Those who find it difficult to lose weight.

JANUARY 19

Let us not become weary in doing good. (Galatians 6:9)

There once was a four-year-old who made the mistake of leaving a door open. The family cat escaped into the dark, unfamiliar outside. The child was chided by her parents as they frantically searched for the pet.

The little girl sat quietly in her room. When she was asked what she was doing, she said, "I'm just tinking good tings." With tears in her eyes, she was trying to do good, to be good, as she waited for the cat to be found. As she did, she asked Jesus to help her parents find the cat.

The end of the story is a happy one. The cat was located. Isn't that just like God?

Do you ever feel like that little girl? You're trying to be good while the tears come flowing. It's enough to make you weary and exhausted in strength, endurance, vigor, and freshness. Yet we're told not to become weary in doing good. What are you supposed to do?

For now, dear child of God, don't be so hard on yourself. You're going through a time of sorrow. If you're weary, don't be surprised.

Try to be like the little girl. Sit down and try to "tink good tings."

Prayer focus for today: Firefighters.

JANUARY 20

Teach us to number our days aright, that we may gain a heart of wisdom. (Psalm 90:12)

What is wisdom? Where can you get it? Do they have capsules of it you can buy at the local health food store? Don't you wish! Does wisdom come along with the school lessons my oldest grand-daughter completes? As she gets older and the academic subjects are more intense, does she become more wise?

Wisdom is found only by walking with the Lord daily. We need to seek his face and be willing to hear what he has to teach us.

We're told to number our days aright. That means each day we are to seek to learn more and more of his truth. When we do this, we will have wisdom. It is an integral part of our being, the heart of our being.

Maybe you don't feel wise during these days of adjustment. Never mind. Just keep focusing on the Lord. His wisdom is more than sufficient for your needs today and forever.

Prayer focus for today: Those whose jobs require them to work nights.

JANUARY 21

Do not conform any longer to the pattern of this world.
(Romans 12:2)

When do you use a pattern? If you have an interest in woodworking, you may use one to cut out a scroll or design. If you're a seamstress, you may need one to make a dress. Young children love to use stencils as patterns to trace designs.

Another way of looking at a pattern is to think of it as a model to follow. We're told in this verse from Romans that we should not follow the pattern or model of this world.

When a loved one dies, the model of this world is quite different from the one Jesus offers us. It's OK to be sad, to mourn, to miss the person, but in Jesus' perfect pattern, we have hope and assurance that all the pieces fit together in his plan for our lives.

Prayer focus for today: Blessings on young people who stand firm in their faith.

JANUARY 22

Glorious and majestic are his deeds. (Psalm 111:3)

L ord, I can see glory and majesty in the rising of the sun and setting of the sun. Your glory and majesty are evident in the mighty roar of the ocean. Your deeds are marvelous.

But, Lord, I'm having a difficult time right now. Tell me what was glorious and majestic about taking my spouse from me. People tell me it was your will. They assure me that you know what is best.

But the nitty gritty of it is simply that the death of my spouse was not a pleasant time. I can see nothing glorious and majestic about dying.

And then you remind me gently of these words from the psalmist. Though your deeds are glorious and majestic, I may not see this fully while my vision is blurred by tears of sorrow.

Just for today, however, I will resolve to stop focusing on myself and my loss. Instead, I will look around this glorious world you created. I will see the clear blue sky overhead. I will feel the sunlight as it shines on me. I will breathe in and revel in the pure wonder of the life you have given me for this time and in this place.

I will then worship the majesty of you!

Prayer focus for today: Blessings on those who hunger and thirst after righteousness.

Rejoice in the Lord always. I will say it again: Rejoice!
(Philippians 4:4)

Walking is an excellent exercise. To encourage this, many shopping malls permit walkers to use them as tracks before the stores open.

My mall-walking days started several years ago. As I walked, the brown tiles on the floor marking the distances, I would see the displays in the windows of the shops over and over again. You know, it was boring!

One day I brought my headset and small tape player. I put praise tapes on and started my usual rounds. To my surprise, my walk was a joy. The next time I walked was also a time of rejoicing, and the next, and the next, until the Lord reminded me, rejoice always.

We are meant to be a praising people! When I walked and only looked at the window displays, the secular things, I was not satisfied. But when I began to praise, my walks were joyful.

Now looking at my situation of singleness in a "secular" mode, I can be dissatisfied. When I rejoice and praise, I approach what the Lord meant me to be.

Prayer focus for today: Girls who suffer from anorexia.

JANUARY 24

Blessed is the man who finds wisdom. (Proverbs 3:13)

A as in apple. B as in boy. These are symbols of how a beginning reader learns to decode words. Have you ever watched or helped a child learn to read? The child struggles, stumbles over words, makes mistakes, then starts over again. It's not always pleasant.

But, in time and with practice, the child can recognize some words right away. By using "word attack skills," they can learn what those letters on the page really mean.

When more and more words become part of the child's recognition, reading becomes almost automatic. From these processes, the child begins to understand written text. The extreme efforts to learn to read are worth it all!

You may be struggling today to learn what the Lord wants to teach you in this situation. Be the child your Abba Father wants you to be.

Start where you are, at the beginning of your understanding. A as in apple. B as in boy.

Prayer focus for today: Patients in hospitals.

For the LORD gives wisdom, and from his mouth come knowledge and understanding. (Proverbs 2:6)

There's an adage that says "when you're talking, you're not learning anything new." It's the same old information, just rehashed. This may be fine when we're talking to God in our prayers. He desires us to be in communication with him.

But communication is a two-way street. To learn new things, to get knowledge and understanding, we need to listen. God is always ready to teach us. Our role is to be still and listen.

It may be more difficult right now at this time of our re-adjustment to do this. We are probably full of prayers like, "What do I do now?" or "How can I muddle through this 'legal' stuff?" We feel so vulnerable. We really need to talk to God and tell him.

And then he reminds us that true knowledge and understanding come from him speaking to us.

Lord, my prayer now is to help me be quiet and listen to you.

Prayer focus today: Those who are deceived by psychics.

JANUARY 26

Be transformed by the renewing of your mind.
(Romans 12:2)

A re you content with the way you are today, right now? Or are there areas of your life that you would like to change? In other words, do you want to be changed? Made over? Transformed?

No one is going to wave a magic wand over you and *poof*—you're what you want to be. It's not that the Lord isn't capable of doing that. It's just that he wants us to look at ourselves, see what's needed, and then work on it!

He asks us for an attitude change. The word here is "renewing" of your mind. That means a new, alternative way of thinking.

If we're in a rut of "why me?" we need to renew our thinking. If we feel hopeless, an adjustment in our attitude is what is called for.

Prayer focus for today: Families who are forced to live in inner cities.

The LORD works out everything for his own ends.
(Proverbs 16:4)

What attracts people to mystery stories? Maybe it's the thrill of the chase or of trying to figure out the solution before it becomes evident. Maybe it's the satisfaction of seeing the criminal get his just reward. Maybe it's the fact that all the loose ends are tied up and by the final page everything ends up well. Don't we wish the circumstances of our lives could be solved in such a neat and tidy way?

In a sense, solutions for us *are* available in a neat and tidy way. We're told that the Lord works out everything. We may say, "Fine, but I'd rather he had done it another way." And then we're reminded that he works out everything for his own ends.

His is the perfect solution. Even if we don't appreciate or understand the mystery story of our lives, still he is providing the answers. All we have to do is hold on until the final page is reached.

Prayer focus for today: Unity in the body of Christ.

JANUARY 28

"Come, let us go up to the mountain of the LORD."
(Isaiah 2:3)

The mountain is so steep, Lord. I just don't think I can do it. I can't really climb that far!

Maybe you've felt that way. Maybe today you feel like a gargantuan mountain looms in your life. Helpless. Hopeless.

The Lord knows how you feel. He is eager for you to come up to his mountain and to reach up to him. If you feel you can't, he provides a cable car for you.

If you've ever been in a cable car going up the side of a steep incline, you probably know there are several factors. You have to be *willing* to step into it and you have to *trust* that the cables are strong enough to hold it.

Once you take the step and enter the car, you go up the mountain. What breathtaking views! What elation when you reach the top! It was worth it all!

So, if you face mountains today, reach out for the cable car. It is strong enough to hold you. He wants you to come up to his mountain.

Prayer focus for today: Students learning English as a second language.

You are my hiding place; you will protect me from trouble and surround me with songs of deliverance. (Psalm 32:7)

Do you ever wish you could just run away, go into hiding somewhere, and leave your troubles of grief, fear, and sorrow behind?

The Lord wants to be your hiding place. He is ready with his mighty open arms to take you up into his lap, let you snuggle as a child, and cover you with his cherishing love. He wants to show you he is your perfect Father.

When you do that, when you turn to him as a child, he protects you from your troubles such as grief, fear, and sorrow. Their pain cannot touch you. Your Father covers you with his perfect care within his hiding place.

When you do this, you will find songs filling your soul. These songs are born of your thankfulness to him for his Fatherly care.

Prayer focus for today: Pilots who air-lift supplies to missionaries.

JANUARY 30

When I called, you answered me; you made me bold and stouthearted. (Psalm 138:3)

When we ask God for something, there are three possible answers: yes, no, or wait.

Receiving the answer of yes really makes us happy. We are told in his word that when we ask for bread, he does provide. He is our Abba Father and all's right with the world. We are content.

But what happens when we call to him and his answer is no? Just before my spouse died, I prayed for his recovery. The Lord's answer was, "No." That answer did not make me feel content.

Sometimes he answers, "Wait." I pray for solutions to what I should do now and he says, "wait." It's hard to be told "no" or "wait."

But I'm finding that those answers are what strengthen me. How could I reach out to another widowed person if the Lord's answers had been different? How could I assure someone that I really trust the Lord if he hadn't asked me to "wait" for his answers?

Praise God for all his answers, whether I understand them or not!

Prayer focus for today: Single fathers of preschool children.

For I will pour water on the thirsty land, and streams on the dry ground. (Isaiah 44:3)

Those restaurants that offer free refills on their sodas, coffee, or tea are just great! On a hot day, when you're really thirsty, you can ask for as many glasses of whatever. Often the server will come around and fill your glass even before you ask.

This abundance of free refills can be a reminder to us of God's promises that he will fill our needs. He tells us that he will pour water on the dry ground.

Maybe you're feeling "dry and thirsty" for the assurance that he really does care about you in your time of sorrow. Cling to his promise in this passage. Even if you're in a period of prolonged dryness, he still promises to provide the vital water for your soul.

Prayer focus for today: Runaways.

FEBRUARY 1

We are weak, but you are strong! (1 Corinthians 4:10)

During these days of being alone, it may be easy to think only of human frailty and weakness. Some books on the subject of widowhood tell us to remember how fragile we are, especially at this time.

These things may be true. In fact, being a Christian can remind us of our weaknesses. But there's more to the picture. One good way to think of this situation is to consider the children's song, "Jesus Loves Me."

Children sing, "I am weak, but he is strong!"

How Scriptural that is!

They continue, "Yes, Jesus loves me. Yes, Jesus loves me."

How Scriptural that is, too!

When you feel less than strong, sing that children's song and let yourself be strengthened in him.

Yes, Jesus loves *you!*

Prayer focus for today: Those who have suffered a devastating fire.

In all your ways acknowledge him. (Proverbs 3:6)

At one time, I lived on the fringe of my favorite Christian radio station's broadcasting area. I purchased the best receiver I could find, and tuned it as finely as I could. Sometimes the broadcast would come in clearly, and I could enjoy the music and all of my favorite teachings. Other times, there would be interference from other radio stations. Hard rock would do its best to crowd out the gospel music and messages. To hear my station, I had to really listen hard and pay close attention.

It's like that in our lives, too. We do our best to tune into the Lord. But there's always interference waiting to overtake our attention. We really have to pay close attention to seek Jesus in all our ways with all of our being.

Maybe it's more difficult for us to do this at this time of our lives. That's OK. All we're asked to do is continue to focus on Jesus the best we can.

Soon, we will find we're focusing on him in all our ways and at all times.

Prayer focus for today: Supreme Court.

FEBRUARY 3

> *But as for me, I will always have hope; I will praise you*
> *more and more.* (Psalm 71:14)

Do people ask, "How are you *really* doing?" Do they give you pitiful looks as they marvel, "I can't imagine being alone"? They act like being bereaved is some sort of plague! Their attempts to understand and comfort fail miserably. It's tough enough without all the well-meaning spreaders of gloom and doom.

Especially in times like these, we should look to the Scriptures for comfort and advice. We're reminded that we will always have hope and the key to that hope is praising God.

Therefore, the way for us to work our way out of grief is to focus on the Lord and praise him. As we praise him more and more, those well-meaning spreaders of gloom and doom will look at us in wonder and see for themselves how great our God really is.

Prayer focus for today: Church groups for senior citizens.

"Submit to God and be at peace with him; in this way prosperity will come to you." (Job 22:21)

I magine that you are a piano. You want to make pleasant music, but what is necessary for this to occur? You have lots of strings inside of you, and these strings must be aligned and in tune before harmonic music is possible. How are they put into tune? They need to be stretched and made taut so the tones will be crisp and clear.

OK. Your piano strings are stretched and in tune. How can music come out of you? Somehow, the keys have to be pounded to strike the strings and make the music. In short, you have to subject yourself to being stretched and pounded to produce what you were built to do.

Can you think of your *life* as being somewhat like that piano? Just as the piano submits to being tuned, we need to submit to God. Only when we do this, can we have his perfect peace and prosperity.

Especially now, we need to submit to him and let him tune us as he sees fit. Our bereavement may be part of the process of his plan. All we're called to do is to let him work his plan for us.

Prayer focus for today: Children with severe hearing loss.

FEBRUARY 5

"I will repay you for the years the locusts have eaten."
(Joel 2:25)

Several years ago, the Lord made it clear to my son-in-law and daughter that they were to leave Southern California. He told them simply to move across the country to the east coast.

After pricing truck rentals, they felt it wisest to rent just a trailer and tow what they could fit into it. As they packed the trailer, they realized it didn't hold nearly as much as they had hoped. Thus, they were forced to get rid of the majority of their household belongings. They had to call in dealers of used furniture and others who make their living by the misfortunes of other people. The Lord assured my son-in-law and daughter that he would repay what the "locusts" had eaten.

The end of this story is a happy one. Since they moved east, the Lord has restored to them many times over what the locusts devoured, and he shows evidence that he intends to bless them with ever greater abundance.

In the same way, dear child of God, he will make up for what the locusts of widowhood have robbed you of. Just listen for his directions to follow.

Prayer focus for today: Translators who are working to put the Word into all languages of the world.

FEBRUARY 6

And the God of all grace . . . will himself restore you and
make you strong, firm and steadfast. (1 Peter 5:10)

The little boy and his father set up a toy train.
They had all the tracks, buildings, and switches.
With great pride and care, they placed the toy engine
on the track, and they coupled all the rail cars that
would form their train. It was ready!

With great anticipation, they turned on the
power and watched as the tiny locomotive started to
pull its load. It went slowly at first, then faster and
faster, until it came to a turn. Off the track it went,
crashing into a tiny village.

Carefully, the father put the train back on the
track, and mended the village buildings. When he
saw that all was well, he let the train start again,
slowly at first.

Our God is like that boy's father. He set up and
orchestrated our lives in much the same way. He lets
us go, but keeps a watchful eye on where we're going.
When we err and go "off track," he himself is there
to restore us and set our path aright.

He's there right now watching you and me, ready
to restore our peace even in our sorrow to make us
strong, firm, and steadfast.

Prayer focus for today: Those who are HIV positive.

FEBRUARY 7

Let us then approach the throne of grace with confidence, so that we may receive mercy and find grace to help us in our time of need. (Hebrews 4:16)

The children of Israel worshipped in a tabernacle set up where they wandered in the desert. An important part of this tabernacle was the Holy of Holies, a sacred place where the priests—the Levites—had the authority to offer sacrifices to the holy God.

With the New Testament covenant, each believer has the authority to approach the throne of grace. We can enter this Holy of Holies by the Blood of the Lamb, our Lord Jesus Christ. What a blessing this is. We can enter into the very throne room of God when we truly are his children, born again and washed in the blood. Hallelujah!

When we come into his presence, we have his assurance that he will grant us mercy because his Son, Jesus himself, is sitting on the throne. As we near the Holy of Holies, Jesus knows our need. He knows our sorrows. He understands fully since he walked the path of a human.

So, dear child of God, approach the throne of grace with a joyful and expectant heart.

Prayer focus for today: Those who feel unloved.

FEBRUARY 8

"Walk in all the ways I command you, that it may go well with you." (Jeremiah 7:23)

When I'm in an unfamiliar area, I always drive with a road map on the seat beside me. Frequently, I'll plan my route and highlight it on the map so I can keep myself apprised of the territory at all times.

Several years ago, I had to travel around the District of Columbia and wend my way into the suburban northern Virginia. For about two months, I had to make this same trip once a week for meetings.

After a few weeks of driving with the map beside me, I felt sure I knew where I was going. So one day I left the map at home. I arrived at the meeting on time, but many others were very late. A truck carrying hazardous cargo had overturned on the very road I had traveled. Fortunately, I was a few minutes early and had missed the accident. If it had happened before I went through, I would have been totally lost without my map. God was watching over me even though I was careless.

That experience taught me to always be prepared with directions, no matter how swell-headed I may be about what I presume to know. It also reminded me to follow the directions of the Lord no matter what circumstances I'm in, even working my way through grief.

Prayer focus for today: Parent/teacher organizations.

FEBRUARY 9

> *As the mountains surround Jerusalem, so the* LORD
> *surrounds his people both now and forevermore.*
> (Psalm 125:2)

Jerusalem always has been and always will be cherished by our God. He chose to nestle it inside the safety of several hills.

The terrain there is very mountainous. The Lord situated the city so skillfully that as you approach it, you don't see Jerusalem until you are startled by being almost upon it. His mountains truly surround his city.

Dear child of God, *you* are God's own, also. Just as he chose to protect Jerusalem by surrounding it with mountains, he chooses to surround you with protections only *he* is capable of providing.

If you feel particularly vulnerable today, that's all right. Just close your eyes; picture him surrounding you with his mountains and his hedge of protection.

And then, give him praise!

Prayer focus for today: Surgeons who hold lives in their hands.

You will be secure, because there is hope; you will look about you and take your rest in safety. (Job 11:18)

One of the classic representations of restfulness is lying in a hammock. In this picture, the hammock is suspended by ropes between two very stalwart and shady trees. The sky is blue above, and the grass is green beneath. There's probably a glass of ice-cold lemonade in the picture as well. What a place to just lie back, relax, and feel secure.

As nice as this picture is, there's a greater peace and security available to those who are the Lord's children. If you want to continue to use the hammock as your picture of the Lord's caring for you, think of the trees that support it. They are the Truth and Righteousness of our God. The hammock itself can represent the Lord Jesus Christ who holds us up. The green grass and blue sky are reminders of the world the Lord has created for us. The lemonade represents him reviving us daily.

Dear child of God, especially today, relax and let the Lord hold you up in his loving arms.

Prayer focus for today: Those who have lost their homes.

42

All Scripture is God-breathed and is useful for teaching, rebuking, correcting, and training in righteousness. (2 Timothy 3:16)

There is a supposition among some Christians that the Bible was all right for when it was written, but surely it was not meant for today. Some classes study the Bible as literature, just an assortment of stories. A question for each true believer, then, is "Where do I stand on this issue?"

There's an answer to that question right there in the Bible. It tells us that Scripture is *God-breathed.* Could that possibly mean that God spoke only to the ancient Hebrews and believers living in the times of the New Testament? I think not! God continues to speak to his children. One of the ways he speaks to us is through his love letter to us, the Bible.

He tells us, too, that *all* Scripture is from him. This does not mean that the Bible merely *contains* the word of God. The Bible *is* the word of God.

Our task as believers is to read all of the word of God. In it we find instruction, encouragement, and solace to help us live our lives more fully in him.

Prayer focus for today: Church music directors.

Lean not on your own understanding. (Proverbs 3:5)

Swimming and jumping into ocean waves is great sport! True ocean lovers relish the thought of "surf's up" and will seek beaches where the waves come crashing onto the sand.

All this is fine, as long as the swimmers are sure they are safe. The problem is that the backwash or undertow can be dangerous. There can be riptides that cut across the water and are real threats to one's safety. Those who are most prudent seek a beach protected by lifeguards. If this is not possible, the wise at least do not go in alone.

In other words, wise swimmers do not lean on their own understanding. The water may beckon, "come in." They may have been at the beach a thousand times before, but need the advice and warning of others.

As believers, we too are cautioned not to lean on our own understanding. We surely cannot do this and make sense of our being widowed. We are called to trust solely in the perfect wisdom of our God. He will make it all clear to us.

Prayer focus for today: Those who have been abandoned.

FEBRUARY 13

Be at rest once more, O my soul, for the LORD has been good to you. (Psalm 116:7)

Since your spouse died, do you feel that your very soul is in a state of unrest? You want to feel at peace. You would like to feel settled, but it's impossible to concentrate on things. Maybe you are forgetful. Maybe you can't sit still. Maybe you just sit too much and don't have the desire to do anything. It's a yo-yo existence.

Our Lord speaks to our soul in his word. He tells us to be at rest, be peaceful, and remember how good he has been to us.

We may say, "That's fine, but I still can't concentrate, can't sleep, can't . . ."

Well then, we need to see what we *can* do. We *can* take a deep breath and say thanks to the Lord for our life. We *can* talk to our Lord and ask him for peace just for the next few minutes.

When we do what we can, step by step, we'll soon be strong enough to tackle what we think we can't do today.

Prayer focus for today: Third World countries.

Perfect love drives out fear. (1 John 4:18)

Valentine's Day. Have you seen enough lacy hearts? Is the mere sight of Valentine candy enough to make you ill? It's tough being in the middle of a society where everyone assumes you are part of a loving couple.

And there's the television programming. This time of year, talk shows feature couples who just love each other. Situation comedies focus on lovey-dovey sweethearts. When the characters in those episodes begin to joke about their sex life, I zap them with my remote control and walk outside to get a breath of fresh air.

Romance does have its place, but right now it's difficult to take.

Then the Lord reminds me in his word about perfect love. The Lord's love for me is the only *perfect* love there is. He reminds me that he alone can be my true Valentine. He is steadfast and loves me more than any mortal could understand.

So, I breathe in the fresh, cool air, look up at the stars, and say, "Thank you, Jesus, for being my Valentine!"

Prayer focus for today: That God be glorified in your life.

FEBRUARY 15

I want to know Christ and the power of his resurrection. (Philippians 3:10)

When driving long distances on interstate highways, you often find the most efficient way to stop for food is to look for signs at the various exits. Once you've selected the restaurant, you pull off the interstate and into the parking lot.

You get out of your vehicle, stretch a little, and go inside to order. As you sit there eating your burger and fries, you may notice you are only one of many who seem to be just passing through. This is just a stop on the way to your final destination.

Do you sometimes feel that way about this earthly life? This is not your final destination. This is only a stopping place. You're just "passing through."

Our final destination is the heavenly home he has prepared for those of us who believe in his name. Even if our way seems bleak at times of our lives, we have the assurance that our final home will be far better than what is going on now.

Amen!

Prayer focus for today: Those who are studying to keep up with technology requirements for their jobs.

When anxiety was great within me, your consolation brought joy to my soul. (Psalm 94:19)

Anxiety can be defined as an "apprehensive uneasiness over an impending or anticipated distress." Before my husband died, I had waves of anxiety at times. I would think, "What would I do if he weren't here anymore?" He and I had talked fleetingly about what each would do if something happened to the other.

But then when something did happen to him, my anxiety level became incredible. I walked into that hospital a wife. I walked out a widow. Yes, I was anxious!

The days immediately after his death were filled with one crisis after another. But the Lord demonstrated his consolations to me in unbelievable ways. He carried me through inconceivable events. He showed me how much he cared. He grieved with me.

And the sequel to that time is that a joy beyond all measure settled upon me and lifted my anxious thoughts.

Praise him!

Prayer focus for today: School dropouts.

FEBRUARY 17

"They will live in safety, and no one will make them afraid." (Ezekiel 34:28)

Have you ever noticed the quantity and variety of night lights that are available today? Some have cartoon characters or flowers, and other even emit aromas. It can give you a clue as to how many children need the security of having a light on at night.

Why are night lights necessary? Fear is the overwhelming reason. Children imagine there are many things that might hurt them. They feel that if they have a light in the room, they are safe. So they sleep, sometimes for years, with a night light.

As children mature in their knowledge of the Lord and Savior, Jesus Christ, they begin to see that the only true safety is in him. Any danger that is a true threat will not be daunted by a little night light. Our *true* safety is found in the name of Jesus which drives out and tramples any potential danger to us.

Dear child of God, especially now if fears of being alone are robbing you of your feeling of safety, cling to the name of Jesus!

Prayer focus for today: Those in depression.

FEBRUARY 18

Show me the way I should go, for to you I lift up my soul. (Psalm 143:8)

You're driving down a road. You're confident you know where you're going. The surroundings are familiar. You have one of your favorite tapes playing. Unexpectedly, there's a fork in the road. You hadn't planned on that!

Sound like the time you lost your spouse? Things were going along as well as humans can do. You knew where you were headed, and pow, a fork in the road appears. You hadn't planned on *that!*

At this fork, you can either decide for yourself which way to go, or you can consult the road map, the perfect road map: Jesus. Ask him for directions. Ask with all your soul!

He will point out the way he chose for you. He had his reasons for putting you here in the first place. Trust him at any other crossroads, forks in roads, or detours you may face.

Prayer focus for today: Counselors who work with troubled children.

FEBRUARY 19

Cast all your anxiety on him because he cares for you.
(1 Peter 5:7)

There's a legend about flowers that were at the foot of the cross where Jesus was crucified. His precious blood flowed down, onto them, making spots on their petals. The flowers were so distressed, they hung their little heads in sorrow. These flowers, the legend tells us, are pansies.

So, dear child of God, picture a bed of pansies encircling the foot of the cross. The Lord asks us to lay our burdens and anxieties there. Can you now picture covering your cares in that bed of colorful pansies? When you do that, anxieties are lost and covered over in what Jesus has done for you by taking away all your sins.

So don't continue to drag those cares around with you. Your Savior shed his blood to take them away. Give him the honor of leaving those cares at the foot of his now-empty cross. Leave them—bury them in the flower bed of pansies.

Prayer focus for today: Blessings on teenagers who have chosen purity before marriage.

Do not add to what I command you and do not sub-tract from it, but keep the commands of the LORD your God that I give you. (Deuteronomy 4:2)

Now that I am widowed, everybody has advice. "You should do this." "Don't do that." "My sister did this, so you should, too."

It's too much! I can't even decide which number to order at a fast food restaurant. How can I ever be sure of any decision I make?

The Lord's word reminds me that in my *own* strength, I can't be sure of any decision. And I can't rely on anyone's human strength alone. Only the commands of the Lord are reliable.

He tells me not to add or subtract from his commands. By reading his word and meditating on it, I *will* understand what he's so eager to tell me.

His advice is all I need. He'll tell me what to do and when to do it. And he's eager to do the same for you!

Prayer focus for today: Integrity in the workplace.

FEBRUARY 21

We will shout for joy when you are victorious and will lift up our banners in the name of our God. (Psalm 20:5)

As we read these words, we can almost feel that we are participants in an athletic contest in an amphitheater. The crowds shout for joy when we score a goal. They even hold up placards of encouragement.

Did you know that this sort of cheering goes on for us in heaven? We're told in the Scriptures (Heb. 12:1) of the "great cloud of witnesses" that surround us. This cloud of witnesses are those who have gone on ahead of us to be in heaven with the Lord. From there, they are cheering us on as we continue our scuffles with the ways of the world.

We can almost hear their shouts of "Bravo!" when we overcome despair. We can almost see them waving pom-poms and cheering, "They did it!" when we rise above our sorrows and praise the Lord wholeheartedly.

So, when you are tempted to sink into the doldrums of mourning, look up to the clouds overhead and wave to your cheering section.

Prayer focus for today: Children in Mother's Day Out programs.

FEBRUARY 22

"Now then, stand still and see this great thing the LORD *is about to do before your eyes!"* (1 Samuel 12:16)

When we're rushing around in a frenzy, we aren't giving the Lord a chance to communicate with us. But communicating with us is his desire.

Do you find yourself in more of a frenzy since your spouse died? After all, there's so much to take care of *by yourself.* There are the utility bills to pay, the car to maintain, the house to clean, the taxes, and the . . . These are enough to keep you pacing back and forth.

The Lord is aware of all those endless details. And he knows what is best for you. He tells us in his word to "stand still," for it is only when we stop our frantic activities that we can be in a position to see what the Lord is going to do for us. We need to be quiet and calm so he can get our attention.

Stand still before him. The agenda of "must do's" can wait.

Be still!

Prayer focus for today: Public school teachers.

FEBRUARY 23

"No one is near to comfort me, no one to restore my spirit." (Lamentations 1:16)

No one really understands how you feel when you lose a spouse. They may say all the "right" words and do all the "expected" things, but no one can restore your joy.

No one? There is One who understands you better than you understand yourself. That One is the God of the universe who made *you* in his image. He made you, so he must have made you with the potential for having these feelings.

When you feel that people don't understand you, or can't comfort you, or let you down, remember the One who will never let you down. He loves you so much because you are his child. His comfort is endless. He will restore your soul with exquisite perfection.

Thanks be to him, the comforter and restorer of your spirit!

Prayer focus for today: Strength for those who are weak in their faith.

Give thanks in all circumstances, for this is God's will
for you in Christ Jesus. (1 Thessalonians 5:18)

Lord, you tell me to give thanks in all circumstances. I read that often in your word. Before
my spouse died, I may have waxed eloquently to others on that very subject. It was so easy to give advice!

But now, I see circumstances in quite another
dimension. It's difficult to give thanks now that I am
alone. How can I be thankful that I must go on in
this life without a partner? Lord, do you really
expect me to be thankful that my spouse is dead?

Then you remind me that you *do* want me to be
thankful in *all* circumstances. You want me to do this
because of what your Son Jesus Christ did for me.
His atoning death on the cross is sufficient and worthy of my thanks, no matter what! When I have a
heart full of gratitude to Jesus, there's no room for
self-pity.

This, then, is your will for me. Thank you, Lord!

Prayer focus for today: Relief from physical pain.

FEBRUARY 25

Let the righteous rejoice in the LORD *and take refuge in him; let all the upright in heart praise him!* (Psalm 64:10)

Do you like taking pictures? I mean the still photographs rather than the action of video recorders. Using your camera for focusing on a subject and then taking the perfect picture can be satisfying.

The photograph itself is still. What you see in that picture is dormant. It's as if the activity were suddenly frozen in time.

Maybe your life today feels like that still picture. Once you were part of the action that could be videotaped. Now that you are bereaved, your life is in a state of suspended animation. The excitement is gone. It's a flat photograph.

What can you do to restore the animation in your life? Rejoice in the Lord, dear child of God. He tells us to take refuge in him and praise him. These actions of taking refuge and praising are exercises for restoring yourself into vibrant living once again. When we do that, we will move out of the still picture mode and into the animated status he desires for us.

Prayer focus for today: Those who report the news through the media.

The LORD is close to the brokenhearted and saves those who are crushed in spirit. (Psalm 34:18)

As we were changing from childhood to adolescence to adulthood, we were encouraged to grow up and be mature. When we reached adulthood, we were probably so conditioned by all that encouragement that we felt we really were big people now instead of children. We were grown up. We could handle life. We were self-sufficient.

When all goes well, it's relatively easy to feel that way. Sure, life has its little glitches, but all in all, we can handle things.

But then something catastrophic happens, like the death of your spouse. Suddenly you're brokenhearted. Your spirit is crushed. You don't feel mature anymore. Maybe you don't even want to be a grown-up.

Take heart, dear child of God. The mighty One of Israel tells us that he is close to the brokenhearted. This means he *is* close to you now more than he was when you felt self-sufficient.

So, give him praise for showing you how close you are to him at this time.

Prayer focus for today: Those in authority over churches.

FEBRUARY 27

He is my loving God and my fortress, my stronghold and my deliverer, my shield, in whom I take refuge. (Psalm 144:2)

When you go out into a rainstorm, there's one thing that's certain. You will get wet unless you plan ahead. Part of that is to take an umbrella with you or keep one in the car or store one at the office, just in case the rains come.

The umbrella is your protection against the inclement weather. You hold it over your head and the rain falls on it rather than on you. The rain water may run over the umbrella and splash down the edges, but when you're inside the main body of the umbrella, you are safe. In a sense, when under an umbrella, you have refuge.

But we have a much more important and real refuge: our loving God is a refuge for us. He is our stronghold to protect us from the world that is inclement. All around us can be perils or the foul weather of sorrow, despair, and self-pity. Our Abba Father is there to provide perfect protection for his children.

Prayer focus for today: Women who have had miscarriages.

FEBRUARY 28

I rise before dawn and cry for help; I have put my hope in your word. (Psalm 119:147)

What is the definition of a habit? It is an action we do so often that it becomes involuntary. Habits can be classified as good or bad. When we are born-again Christians, one response to our salvation is trying to expand our good habits.

One of the best habits is the practice of daily devotions. This is a time of reading and meditating on the word of God. It is a time of praying. Though the time of day can vary from person to person, the most important aspect is that devotions are done daily.

The psalmist suggests that he rose early for a time of devotions. We can surmise from the psalms that parts of his time was devoted to songs of praise. We can see from his writings that his early morning meditations included delving into the Word.

Whatever time of day you choose, be sure to make it a habit. It is especially important to you at this time of re-adjusting your life.

Prayer focus for today: Those who are bound by the past.

FEBRUARY 29

"Salt is good, but if it loses its saltiness, how can you make it salty again? Have salt in yourselves, and be at peace with each other." (Mark 9:50)

Once when my children were small, I was rushing to make cookies from scratch. Hurriedly I mixed the flour, sugar, and other ingredients. I shaped the cookies, sprinkled them with little candies, and baked them until they were the perfect color. Carefully, I took them off the baking sheet and let them cool. Whew! Job done!

We tasted the cookies. Though they looked great, they tasted terrible. They had no specific flavor; they were bland. I realized then that I had forgotten one ingredient: salt. Even though the recipe only called for one quarter teaspoon of it, it was surprising how the omission of such a tiny amount of salt made such a difference in the final result.

But it shouldn't have surprised me, really. The Scriptures tell us of the many attributes of salt. We're told that it is good. We're to be salt in the world. We are to have salt in ourselves and be at peace with each other.

Right now, dear child of God, resolve to be the ingredient that the Lord has called you to be in the world.

Prayer focus for today: Workers on road crews.

The oil of joy for mourning. (Isaiah 61:3 KJV)

In the Old Testament covenant, oil was used for its curative effects. It was also used as a cosmetic. The anointing of one for sacred duties was done with oil.

The oil in the New Testament covenant is symbolic of the Holy Spirit. With his exquisite sensitivity, the Lord assures us that he is eager to give us the "oil of joy for mourning." In other words, he knows all about our grieving. He understands our sorrow. He wants to pour his oil of joy over us.

His is not ordinary oil, but a fragrant, soothing substance that penetrates our entire being. Imagine having it poured over you, absorbing it, the oil becoming part of you. Experience in your mind the oil being gently stroked into your soul. It is the oil from the Lord. It is his Holy Spirit!

Today, as we are in this time of our bereavement, we need to reach up to his Holy Spirit and let him fill our emptiness with his perfect oil of joy.

Prayer focus for today: Courage to tell others about Jesus.

MARCH 2
"The righteous will live by faith." (Galatians 3:11)

No one is really comfortable driving in fog. The gray mist is all around you and you have to concentrate to be able to move with any amount of safety. But one thing I have noticed is that it's a little easier to drive in the fog at night. When it's dark, you are certain that all the cars will have their headlights on, and there are street lights which help you know where you are in relation to where you've come and where you're going.

Maybe today you're feeling like you're in a nighttime fog. Since you have been widowed, your life seems desolate and gray. Remember the street lights? They help to show you the way. They help you determine your location. They can point out where you are in relation to where you're going.

Now, look at our verse for today: "The righteous will live by faith." The righteous person is one who is in right relation with God. So if your life seems to be dark and foggy, ponder where you are in relation to him. He will provide the answers to help you find your way. Have faith in him.

Prayer focus for today: Nurses who volunteer at medical missions.

*May the L*ORD *answer you when you are in distress; may the name of the God of Jacob protect you.* (Psalm 20:1)

Now that you're widowed, you may feel vulnerable. You may have the feeling that you're being attacked by seen or unseen enemies. Once there were two of you who were joined. Together you could stave off attacks from the enemy of believers.

What can you do? There's just one of you now. But you have access to the most powerful source in the universe. That is the Name of the God of Jacob. Just mentioning the Name of God scatters the host of enemies that try to attack you. Those enemies called doubt, fear, loneliness, and anger all shudder and disappear when you rebuke them in the powerful Name of the Lord.

Cling to the Name. Claim the might of the Name. Let the Name protect you!

Prayer focus for today: Counselors in crisis pregnancy centers.

MARCH 4

Your ways, O God, are holy. What god is so great as our God? You are the God who performs miracles. (Psalm 77:13–14)

Lord, I agree with these words. You *are* holy. You *are* my great God. You *are* a God who performs miracles.

But, Lord, I don't understand why you didn't perform a miracle and heal my spouse. Didn't I ask? Didn't my fellow believers also plead with you? Didn't my spiritual leaders claim healing for my spouse in your name? I don't understand.

And then you come to me, ever so gently, and remind me of your great power. I need to be still and know you are great. You *do* perform miracles.

When I asked for a miracle to save my spouse from dying, you had an even greater miracle in mind. It is all part of your perfect plan for my spouse, for me, and for your work in your world.

Help me to rest in this!

Prayer focus for today: Singles' groups.

65

He will make your paths straight. (Proverbs 3:6)

Have you ever realized how straight most interstate highways are? The rocks and hills are blasted and moved in order to make those super-highways as direct as possible.

Sometimes, however, these interstates circle around a metropolitan area. These roads that should be straight veer off in odd directions.

At one time, I needed to go west on one of these roads. I followed that red, white, and blue sign that said "west." I soon realized that I wasn't going west at all. I was headed east on one of those circumferential highways.

I pulled off and found my way to an older road that I was certain went the direction I needed to go. It was a slower pace than the interstate, but at least I got where I needed to be.

Sometimes, it seems that our path is not what we had planned. Sometimes, we have to go off the main road and travel a lesser known route. If your life seems like that today in your bereavement, look for what the Lord is telling you.

Prayer focus for today: Businesses who strive to make their companies socially responsible.

MARCH 6

You turned my wailing into dancing; you removed my sackcloth and clothed me with joy. (Psalm 30:11)

How did you react upon the death of your spouse? Relief? Shock? Denial? Crying? Wailing?

The children of Israel reacted to death in many observable ways. Wailing was an integral part of their expression of grief. Family and friends gathered and wept vociferously. Sackcloth was the choice of garments next to the skin. This irritated the skin and was a constant reminder of their sorrow. Their times of mourning with these external rituals went on for long periods of time.

What about you? If you're newly bereaved, crying and even wailing can be expected. It is necessary to express your feelings and "get real," to quote the vernacular.

If your bereavement is not so new and you're still wailing, maybe your garment of sackcloth is giving you problems. Perhaps this garment has been self-imposed. Look at the verse from Psalm 30: "*You turned wailing into dancing, you removed my sackcloth and clothed me with joy.*"

The "you," of course, is the Lord. And note that the verbs are past tense. He's already done it. So, grab those tissues, dry your wailing tears, toss out the sackcloth, and receive the utter joy he has for you.

Prayer focus for today: Those who make decisions pertaining to public school curricula.

His faithfulness will be your shield and rampart. You will not fear. (Psalm 91:4–5)

With all our modern methods of national defense, we don't always have a frame of reference for words like "shield," "rampart," or "armor." We're so dependent upon missiles and jets that we don't even think of the armor of God.

Yet the Scriptures are full of images referring to it. Some versions of the Bible even contain little drawings of a soldier clad in armor, ready to tackle seen or unseen enemies.

We're told that the Lord's faithfulness will be our shield, so he must want us to picture his care for us as with armor. Think of it, dear child of God, he wants to be the shield before you to fend off any attacks intended for you.

In our widowed state, these attacks may be the darts of insecurity, sorrow, or anxiety. Whatever the darts are loaded with, our Abba Father is our impervious shield. We need not fear!

Prayer focus for today: Families of those with terminal illnesses.

MARCH 8

"He reached down from on high and took hold of me; he drew me out of deep waters." (2 Samuel 22:17)

Even a brief study of comparative religions demonstrates this basic truth. Christianity is the *only* religion in which God reaches down to meet us and pull us up. In all other religions, their god stays far above mere mortals. The only way to reach these gods is to work your way up. Praise God that our Redeemer loves us so much that he came down to us.

By him seeking us, he has drawn all of us out of the deep waters of our sin that once threatened to swallow us up. Praise him for his wonderful plan of salvation!

Sometimes during worship as I lift my hands in praise, I can almost feel God's motion in my direction as though he wants to touch my fingers with his. I know that in my frail, human form, it is not possible to touch the Holy One, but I feel blessed to know that he is there smiling and loving me.

My hope for you today is that you seek him and reach out for him.

Prayer focus for today: Special blessings on "completed Jews," Hebrews who have realized that Jesus is their long-awaited Messiah.

In you, O LORD, I have taken refuge; let me never be put to shame; deliver me in your righteousness. (Psalm 31:1)

When driving down a highway in a torrential rainstorm, have you ever noticed the relief you feel when you're traveling under an overpass? The pounding water is not there. It's quiet. You may even see grateful motorcyclists staying in that haven as protection from the deluge. Have you ever wished there would be a covering over the entire road?

That may seem absurd, but there are often storms in our lives where a wish such as that is possible to fulfill.

We can be inundated with cares of life that pelt down upon us unmercifully. These cares may be especially poignant in this time of our mourning. We may feel a little like those motorcyclists caught out in the torrent.

But, praise God, our Father is there to be a refuge for us. His deliverance is there for *all* the road, not just at selected overpasses.

Prayer focus for today: Volunteers who work in hospitals.

MARCH 10

*"Come to me, all you who are weary and burdened, and
I will give you rest."* (Matthew 11:28)

I'm so tired, Lord. There used to be two of us to do this. And now it's just me.

Yes, there were two of you to take care of the bills, the kids, the house, and now you feel so intensely alone.

But you're *not* alone. A T-shirt blazes, "I'm single but I'm never alone." No, you are not alone. Jesus is there with you.

If you're tired, bring your weariness to him. If financial burdens concern you, lay them at his feet. If the kids are wearing you down, remember he loves them, too, so yield to him.

He promises to give you rest. True satisfying rest comes only when you turn over all your situations to the One who understands and loves you without abandon.

Prayer focus for today: Christian recording artists.

"Hear my prayer, O Lord, listen to my cry for help; be not deaf to my weeping." (Psalm 39:12)

Have you ever tried to interact with someone who is deaf? You probably soon found that in order to communicate, you had to learn to sign. You had to take the initiative to prepare yourself to be converse with that deaf person.

Is God deaf to us? Or are we the deaf ones? He has taken the initiative to communicate with us by giving us his holy word and his promise of salvation through the atonement provided by his Son becoming flesh. He has, in a sense, learned a language we can understand by becoming like us.

How, then, can we be so audacious to think that God doesn't hear us? He *does* hear our spoken prayers, the cries of our heart, and the thoughts we wish. He understands our weeping and our sorrow totally.

Praise him for his perfect solution to the problem of our deafness.

Prayer focus for today: Boys who lack a steadfast father figure.

MARCH 12
"All things are possible with God." (Mark 10:27)

I just can't go on alone, Lord. I really depended upon my spouse for emotional support. Friends and acquaintances mean well; but Lord, my spouse was my best friend. I just can't go on alone.

And you remind me, "All things are possible with God."

I'll never get over this hurt, this intense void in my heart and soul. When my spouse died, most of me died also because I was so much a part of him. I'll just never get over it.

"All things are possible with God."

What will become of me? I just don't see any future. All the things I worked to attain just don't have any meaning any more. There's nothing to look forward to. . . .

"All things are possible with God."

Prayer focus for today: Our natural resources.

*He turned the desert into pools of water and the parched
ground into flowing springs.* (Psalm 107:35)

In this hour of my life, it's easy to feel dry. Once I
was full. I had a full life and a full marriage. Now
there's desert and parched ground. It's tough to think
beyond this shriveled thing that once was my life.

But he tells me that he turned the desert into
pools of water. He said he "turned" it, past tense.
That means he's already done it. So, why do I still
feel dry?

Maybe it's because I'm still wallowing where I am
today. Maybe it's because I look around and only see
what I perceive as dry.

He tells me again that it has been done. He has
supplied the streams of living waters. My assignment,
then, is to accept those waters and let them work
their miracles by making my arid lands run once
again full of a flowing spring.

Prayer focus for today: Local governing authorities.

MARCH 14

> *"To him who knocks, the door will be opened."*
> (Luke 11:10)

Watch a little toddler trying to figure out a door. She looks at panels on the door, maybe running a tiny finger around the molding. She may try to eat the hardware, thinking maybe that will open the door. She may step back and look up. The door must look at least a hundred times bigger than her. Finally, she beats her little fists on the door. Someone hears and opens it to welcome her.

Are we like the toddler, trying all sorts of ineffectual means to make sense out of our situation? We may ponder, grasp at straws, and panic at how gargantuan the problem is. In desperation we pound our fists just as the toddler does.

It is then that we realize he was there all the time just waiting for us to knock. All we had to do was let him know we're there. Just a gentle tap will do, just a whispered "Lord."

Praise be to God who waits patiently for us to realize how easy it is for us to find him.

Prayer focus for today: Those who have a habit of using foul language.

He heals the brokenhearted. (Psalm 147: 3)

When the doctors came to me and said, "It's over," my heart felt like it had been broken into a million pieces. I went through all the necessary arrangements, and through the tears, I kept trying to comfort those around me.

And now, months later, my heart still isn't intact. Even when I feel parts of it are together, the pain of the loss comes over me at the oddest times, hearing a familiar song, seeing a car on the road that looks just like the one he drove.

Others who have been widowed tell me that the first year is the worst, the second is equally hard, and it gets better after that. But, Lord, it's been longer than that. Will I always be brokenhearted?

Then you remind me of your word. You promise to *heal* the brokenhearted. So, instead of whining and wondering if I'll always be like this, I should look for your healing. When I concentrate on what you promised you'd do, the day-to-day sorrow fades. I look for your total healing of my heart, so I can go forth and be your servant.

Prayer focus for today: That Christians show the Light of Christ to the world.

MARCH 16

He has made everything beautiful in its time.
(Ecclesiastes 3:11)

It is said that beauty is in the eye of the beholder. We look at ourselves in the mirror and we see receding hairlines, pot bellies, and big noses. We never seem to behold beauty in ourselves.

Especially at this time of our lives as we try to re-adjust to the single status, we can be very sensitive to how we look or how we think we look. It's easy when we're in this situation to see only what we consider to be our less attractive features.

But there is one who looks at us and sees perfect beauty. That one is our Creator. So maybe it's an insult to him when we don't appreciate what he has given us. He's also our Abba Father. Any pain we feel about ourselves, he feels even more deeply.

He makes everything beautiful. To him, he beholds us as his enchanting children. To him our beauty is breathtaking. We are his precious ones.

So, the next time you look in the mirror and don't like every feature you see, you need to say, "I'm a King's Kid, so of course I'm beautiful."

Prayer focus for today: Counselors for residents in group homes for the mentally ill.

"But now, Lord, what do I look for? My hope is in you." (Psalm 39:7)

Remember the story of *Goldilocks and the Three Bears?* Goldilocks came into the home of the three bears and looked for all sorts of things. She looked for food, found the porridge, and ate up the little bear's food which was "just right." As she continued into the house, she looked for a chair and a bed, finding something else too hard or too soft before she went on.

Do you feel today as if you're looking, but you don't know what for? Widowhood has a way of keeping us a little off center. We know in our spirits that things aren't right. We just don't know what to do about it.

When we ask our Abba Father to help us look, he is there waiting. He tells us that he knows we feel lost. He knows things we seek may be too hard or too soft. He knows what is just right for us.

He is what is just right for us. Praise him for coming and planning what is best for us.

Prayer focus for today: Women who are exploited.

MARCH 18

You have been given fullness in Christ, who is the head over every power and authority. (Colossians 2:10)

You probably have heard definitions of pessimists and optimists. One of these definitions centers around a glass of liquid that is not filled to capacity. The pessimist sees the glass and says it's half empty. The optimist sees the glass as half full. It's all a matter of how each sees the situation. Same glass, different perspectives.

The Scriptures tell us that we have fullness in Christ. How we perceive that fullness depends upon our outlooks. Maybe when things were going well, before we were bereaved, we could see the fullness as really full. Now we may see the fullness as half empty.

But he is eager for us to receive and really feel the total fullness he offers us in Christ Jesus, Our Savior. He knows it's more difficult for us now, but that doesn't change his desire to fill us with his perfect love.

Just for today, we tell ourselves to only see the glass as half full.

Prayer focus for today: Peace for Israel.

But you are to hold fast to the LORD your God, as you have until now. (Joshua 23:8)

Amusement parks are supposed to amuse you. Some of the rides do just that. On the other hand, some of the rides can be terrifying.

Picture this: you're on one of those loopy-doopy contrivances. You're instructed to hold on to the safety devices, so you do. And the "fun" begins. You speed through the ride. You're twisted and turned. You never know what is coming. All you know is that you're holding on as tightly as you can.

Life can be a lot like the loopy-doopy. We never know what's ahead. All we can do is hang on to our Creator, the Lord God. Maybe your life has been a series of unexpected events. The best thing to do, the only thing you *can* do, is hang on to Jesus.

He has carried his children through worse than this. He can carry you through and into the very gates of Paradise. So keep a firm hold on him today, tomorrow, and forever.

Prayer focus for today: Those with cerebral palsy.

MARCH 20

"My Father will honor the one who serves me."
(John 12:26)

Don't you long to hear the Lord say to you, "Well done good and faithful servant"? It will happen! He promises that his servants will be rewarded.

Maybe you wanted to be his servant but it was not always possible. When you were married, you had to consider your mate's needs and wishes. Perhaps you would have liked to go on a short-term mission trip, but your spouse didn't want you to go. The Lord will bless you for having honored your allegiance to your mate.

Now that you're not married, perhaps he is calling you to become his servant in another area. It's not that he chose to take your spouse so you'd be free to do his will. It's just that he may be asking you to use your new status as a background for other scenes of servanthood for him.

We're promised that he will honor the one who serves him. Whether we serve him locally or globally, he still will honor us. Our task today as singles is to ask him where he wants us and then be obedient to his leading.

Prayer focus for today: Inner city missions.

The LORD God said, "It is not good for the man to be alone. I will make a helper suitable for him." (Genesis 2:18)

Lord, you said right in the beginning of your Book that it's not good to be alone. Does this mean that my new single life is bad? I see older couples together and I feel cheated. At times, I am angry and feel this widowhood is not good at all.

You also said in Genesis that you'd make a helper. Now you've taken that helper away. I don't understand this at all. It's not good to be alone. We all need a helper.

Where is *my* helper?

And then you gently remind me that you are the perfect helper for me. You are the permanent, unfailing helper who is always there.

Prayer focus for today: Those who overextend themselves financially.

MARCH 22

*And the peace of God, which transcends all understand-
ing, will guard you hearts and your minds in Christ
Jesus.* (Philippians 4:7)

It's unbelievable how many details arise at the time of
the death of a spouse and afterward. It's bad enough
to feel unrest in your heart and spirit because of your
bereavement. But you feel unrest in your mind because
of all the things that need to be done.

Probate can be a hassle. Taxes can be a concern.
What to do with personal belongings can be dis-
concerting. Then there are the letters and phone calls
and you have to replay the story of how and when the
death occurred. All these items bog down your heart
and mind. Where is the peace you yearn for?

In the midst of all these details, the only peace that
is lasting is found in our God. He is waiting to grant
his perfect peace to your heart and to your mind.

Prayer focus for today: New believers in Christ.

A cheerful heart is good medicine, but a crushed spirit dries up the bones. (Proverbs 17:22)

When your spouse died, did you feel that your spirit was crushed? Maybe you were so shocked that you felt nothing. That's a crushed spirit. Maybe your sobs were shattering. That, too, is a spirit that is crushed. The Bible describes "dried up bones" as a result of your spirit being crushed. Maybe today in this time of mourning, your spirit still feels dry and empty.

You may wonder whether you will always feel this way. Is a "dried up spirit" part of the way of life of the widowed?

Dear child of God, you do not have to live like this for the rest of your life. Your Abba Father wants more for you. He is eager for your spirit to heal.

He has an antidote for you: a cheerful heart. You may ask then, "How can I be cheerful?" A start toward this is to think of how much God loves you. Then thank and praise him for the salvation offered through Jesus Christ, our Lord. When you begin to praise him, his healing medicine begins to do its work, and you're on your way to repairing your spirit and making your heart a cheerful one.

Prayer focus for today: Habitat for Humanity.

MARCH 24

When I am afraid, I will trust in you. (Psalm 56:3)

The theme song of two of the *Three Little Pigs* was, "Who's Afraid of the Big Bad Wolf? Tra La, La La La." They sang and danced with such bravado. Nothing scared them until the huffing and puffing blew down their houses. It was then they realized how vulnerable they really were. Instead of being intrepid little pigs, they were scared little pigs.

Our adult lives can be a lot like those of the little pigs. We may feel we're invincible, and then the huffing and puffing enters the scene. Sickness comes into our home, death takes our spouse, and we realize how fragile we really are. We become scared little children.

In the eyes of our God, it's probably good when we realize we are children. We're told to come to him. We're told to trust in him completely as a child would. So, when the huffing and puffing winds of affliction blow our way, we need to reach out all the more to our completely sovereign and trustworthy God.

Prayer focus for today: Care-givers in day care centers.

"He will teach us his ways, so that we may walk in his paths." (Isaiah 2:3)

When we have been born again, we have freedom: freedom from the penalty of our sin because we have been washed in the cleansing blood of Jesus Christ our Lord. This is true freedom. But it is not a license to do anything we please. Our God loves us so much that he set up boundaries for our behavior.

Those boundaries have been set by him, the Creator of all. They are his laws as written in his love letter to us, the Bible. He knows us. He knows our strengths. He knows our weaknesses. He knows that we need limits to keep us safe and secure. It is when we operate within these that we are the most content.

And when the trials of life come roaring over us, we can nestle safely within our Lord's safe territory. When sorrow or bereavement tempt us to question, we need only to stay with him. Then we can find contentment in his path.

Prayer focus for today: Those who are deceived by cults.

MARCH 26

Save me, O God, for the waters have come up to my neck.
I sink in the miry depths, where there is no foothold.
(Psalm 69:1–2)

Learning to swim is a good thing. Learning *how* to swim is another matter. It can be an intimidating experience. You're in the water and the instructor tells you to put your face in the water and blow bubbles. Talk about water coming up your neck! Later they try to get you to float on top of it. Just relax and let the water pick you up. Talk about miry depth with no foothold!

But one day, you find yourself blowing bubbles, breathing correctly, floating, kicking, and stroking properly. You're swimming! It doesn't matter how deep the pool is. You don't even need a foothold anymore!

When you truly trust God for your salvation, it's a little like being able to swim. He gives you the ability to lean totally on him and he'll carry you through. No matter what waters threaten you—sorrow, anger, or fear—he'll keep you swimming.

Prayer focus for today: Our court system.

I can do everything through him who gives me strength.
(Philippians 4:13)

Do you enjoy looking through a kaleidoscope? It can be fun watching the patterns of the colored glass change as you rotate it. One minute the pattern may look like a flower; the next it may resemble a stained glass window. In your mind's eye, you can imagine what these varying shapes resemble. They change all the time.

Our lives change constantly, much as the patterns do in the kaleidoscope. Just when we get used to one thing, another comes to take its place. Just when we feel we can do things well, our situation changes.

How has your life changed since the death of your spouse? Do you feel like it's a kaleidoscope, never the same even if you didn't ask for it?

We're told in his word that no matter what the difficulties are, we can do everything through him who gives us strength. So, instead of living in dread of those changes we know are coming, let's look up to him and welcome what he has in store for us!

Prayer focus for today: School bus drivers.

MARCH 28

"The grass withers and the flowers fall, but the word of our God stands forever." (Isaiah 40:8)

There's something depressing about seeing dried-up lawns. Flowers that are shriveled and past their blooming period are also a sad sight. It could make one feel hopeless, that nothing lasts.

Even if those same grass roots become green next season or if those flower stalks send out new shoots that bloom, the cycle continues. None of these last.

Maybe you feel your marriage is like the dry, withered flowers. Once it was beautiful. Now there's nothing left.

It's true, your marriage as you knew it is no more. But there is one thing that you know will never change. We're assured that the word of God stands forever. No circumstances in this life or beyond will change that.

Our God's word is steadfast. This time of adjustment to being single is the ideal time for you to study his word with more fervor and more expectancy. This is where your security can be found. Amen!

Prayer focus for today: Those on disability retirement.

"Then you will know the truth, and the truth will set you free." (John 8:32)

Through the ages, humankind has conjured up many philosophies. But the only truth that matters is that God sent his only Son to redeem those who call on his name as Savior. This is not an idea from humanity, but a profound work of grace born of the infinite wisdom of God. Hallelujah!

Jesus himself said that when you know the truth, you will be free from the penalty of sin, free from guilt, and free from doubt.

Is doubt bothering you right now? Do you wonder if God really cares about you in this widowed situation?

Look again at the words from John 8:32. You know the truth. You recognize that Jesus is God's son. You understand that accepting him as your Savior is your assurance of being part of his kingdom.

When you know, really *know* the truth, it will set you free from doubt, from worry, and from any of the other little annoyances that threaten you in your fragile state of bereavement.

Cling to the one truth you know for certain: Jesus Christ *is* Lord. In this, you will find that you are free.

Prayer focus for today: Those whose addictive behaviors have caused them to be homeless.

MARCH 30

> *"Does the clay say to the potter, 'What are you making?'"* (Isaiah 45:9)

Several years ago, I was in a preschool classroom where the teacher had a terrarium. Inside it she had a very small garter snake. One little boy looked at it and asked me why the snake was the shape it was. I told him that God had made it that way. The child looked up at me and said, "How did he do that? Did he roll him?"

God certainly has full license to roll, pound, or bake the clay, whatever he chooses to do. And *we* are his clay. We may question what he's doing as his gentle hands work to mold us into what he wants. Our questioning doesn't phase him a bit. The Master Potter has a specific form in mind for us, and he'll use whatever means necessary to accomplish it.

Our happy experiences are part of his shaping process. Our less-than-happy experiences are also part of it. Our role is to be pliable despite our feelings and let him work his perfect plan for us.

Prayer focus for today: Those who need to yield completely to the Lord.

But you are a chosen people, a royal priesthood.
(1 Peter 2:9)

How good are you at selecting watermelons? Do you thump? Do you press the blossom end? Do you test the rind? Whatever system you use, you try to choose the best.

Our Lord has also selected the best. He has called *you* to be part of his chosen people. He chose you, set you apart as being very special to him. He did this because from the very beginning of time, as recorded in Genesis, you were made in the image of God.

Since you were chosen by God, you are part of a royal priesthood. You may question that. Not all of us have gone to seminary, so how can we be priests? Being a priest has been defined as being Christ's representative to the world. You may be the only Christ that some people will ever see. That's quite a responsibility! But remember, he has chosen you for this task. He made you, so he must believe that you can do it.

No matter what your outward circumstances are, rejoice that he chose you. He knows you and is waiting for you to show Christ to the world.

Prayer focus for today: Those who must commute to work during rush hours.

APRIL 1

> *"Give thanks to the LORD, call on his name."*
> (Isaiah 12:4)

It's a good thing to give thanks to the Lord. Can we all agree on that? Even when we don't "feel" grateful, it's still a good thing to thank him.

It's also good to call on his Name. If you search the Scriptures you will soon see that God has many names. We know he's our Abba Father. We acknowledge him as Lord. We give glory to him as the Mighty One of Israel. We praise him as Emmanuel, God with us.

Today, at this time of your life, you may want to concentrate on two Old Testament names of God. Both of these names address your specific needs during your time of living with your bereavement.

If you wonder what will happen to you, or you don't think you can make it alone, look to Jehovah-Jireh. This name for God means Jehovah will provide. What a touching name! He promised he'd take care of you.

If you are unsettled in your adjustment, think of him as Jehovah-Shalom. This name for God means peace. What a blessing to you! The Mighty God of Israel offers you peace.

All praise be to Jehovah-Jireh. All praise to Jehovah-Shalom!

Prayer focus for today: Counselors in inner city schools.

And when the Chief Shepherd appears, you will receive the crown of glory that will never fade away. (1 Peter 5:4)

Today there seems to be a lot of disagreement about the mechanics of the second coming of Christ. There are the proponents of a pre-tribulation rapture of the saints. Others champion the cause of being post-trib. Some even take a stand by naming specific dates when events are supposed to occur.

But whenever or however it happens, we can agree that he *is* coming again. He, who is known as our Chief Shepherd, will return for his chosen, born-again saints. These saints who follow him are his sheep.

Sheep are not all that smart. They tend to wander off. They really need to be taken care of.

(Sound like anyone you know?) In time, after being with the shepherd, they do learn to recognize the voice of the shepherd.

Just imagine how marvelous it will be when we hear the voice of our Shepherd calling to us when he comes again. He will call us by name and grace us with a crown of glory that will be eternal.

It won't matter then whether the timing is pre-trib, post-trib, or whatever. All the sorrows and cares of our lives today will be nothing. We will be blessed beyond anything we can imagine now.

Prayer focus for today: Those who are struggling to sell their homes.

APRIL 3

> *Guard my teachings as the apple of your eye.*
> (Proverbs 7:2)

C an we agree that the teachings from the Lord are the words in the Bible? Can we further agree that these words are therefore to be treasured? What do we do with treasures? We take special care of them. We protect them.

He tells us in his word to guard his teachings as the apple of your eye. The apple of your eye is symbolic of something very special to you or the center of your focus.

One good way to take special care of the word of God is to study it. The best way to preserve it is to make it a part of you by committing to memory the portions of the Bible that the Lord directs you to.

You may agree with all of this. You may wish you could do that, but since your spouse died, you just can't concentrate even on reading, much less memorizing! How can you be expected to do this? It's just not possible.

Be gentle with yourself. He understands completely. He knows that when the time is right, you'll be ready. In the meantime, cherish his teachings and thank him for making these words available to you.

Prayer focus for today: Children with learning disabilities.

APRIL 4

"But now I urge you to keep up your courage."
(Acts 27:22)

When your spouse died, you may have turned numb. It's our human way of dealing with shock. You went through all the arrangements and finalities. You were being courageous.

How are you doing now? All the relatives have returned home. The reality that you're alone sinks in. You have to deal with the kids, the finances, the lawn mowing—all by yourself.

This is the time you really need courage. Just like the cowardly lion in *The Wizard of Oz*, we need courage. But remember the story? The lion had the potential to be brave inside him all the time. He just needed an outward sign, a medal for valor.

Pretend you, too, have a medal for courage and keep looking upward to the One who is cheering you on.

Keep up your courage!

Prayer focus for today: Dissenters in the church.

APRIL 5

> *You hear, O LORD, the desire of the afflicted; you encourage them, and you listen to their cry.* (Psalm 10:17)

Not many people like ice storms. The ice covers roads, crossings, and sidewalks. It makes travel difficult and dangerous. It makes us feel afflicted or burdened. What use, then, is an ice storm?

The ice also covers trees and bushes. At first sight, we may assume in our burdened status that this is also an affliction. But look: the moonlight glistens through the ice-covered tree branches. What an exquisite, unexpected delight that is!

That's a little like the way our Lord works to encourage us. The ice storms of our lives are those less-than-pleasant experiences. You may be enduring one of your ice storms right now as you try to cope with your mourning. You may feel afflicted. You *think* the Lord hears your cry, but can you be sure?

And then his clear, luminous moonlight shines through the ice-covered branches. It is his assurance to you that he has heard you. It's his way of encouraging you to look up to him, even in the midst of the ice storm of this particular time.

Prayer focus for today: Teachers who volunteer overseas to educate children of missionaries.

APRIL 6

"In my distress I called to the LORD; *I called out to my God. From his temple he heard my voice; my cry came to his ears."* (2 Samuel 22:7)

Since the death of your spouse, do you find yourself calling out to the Lord more than you did before? In your distress or sorrow, do you seek his face with more eagerness? Then do you question where he really is? How can the God of the universe hear or even care about your pleas?

Our answer is found throughout his love letter to us, the Bible. He does hear. He does listen. He does care. He gives us positive affirmations of that in this verse.

As mere humans, we may wonder how he can hear us. After all, he is the Lord. He must dwell in a magnificent place, a temple. But he assures us that he can. He further assures us that we can approach him in that temple. His residence may be in the Holy of Holies, but he has provided a way for us to enter that sacred place.

The way was by the Blood of the perfect sacrifice, the Blood of Jesus Christ. Praise God for his plan and for his making a way for us to approach him and be heard.

Prayer focus for today: Parents of children with spina bifida.

APRIL 7

> *"Look at the birds of the air; they do not sow or reap or store away in barns, and yet your heavenly Father feeds them."* (Matthew 6:26)

Bird feeders are really in. Go to any garden store and you'll see all sorts of inventive ways to feed our feathered friends. Grocery stores sell huge sacks of wild bird seed, sunflower seeds, and cracked corn. Suburbanites carry these bags home in their mini-vans and store up those large sacks for when it's needed.

They fill the feeders and, unless there are neighborhood cats, the birds swarm around the feeder blissfully satiating their appetites. They are totally oblivious to the steps that were necessary to get that seed to the feeder and to them. The birds did not go to the grocery store and carry the sacks of feed and yet it's there for them.

Could it be that our heavenly Father cares for us in the same way? Could it be that we are frequently oblivious to the painstaking steps he takes to provide for us?

Prayer focus for today: Those who are trying to overcome the habit of smoking.

APRIL 8

"Do not be terrified; do not be discouraged, for the
Lord your God will be with you wherever you go."
(Joshua 1:9)

It's easy to feel like a fifth wheel when you find your-self single again. It seems the world is set up for even numbers of people. Restaurants have tables for two or four. Hotels offer specials on a couple's weekend. I'm frequently asked, "Will your husband be joining you?" I choke back the tears and shake my head.

Lord, where are you in all of this? I don't want to be in the way, but it sure is easy to be discouraged. Will I always feel like an extra person?

And then you remind me that you, my God, will be with me wherever I go. To you, I'm not a fifth wheel. To you, I am your special child. With you, I am totally accepted. With you, I am not alone.

Praise you for showing me that you are right here beside me no matter where or what my situation is.

Prayer focus for today: Christian teachers in public school.

APRIL 9

"For in him we live and move and have our being."
(Acts 17:28)

R emember Pinocchio, the marionette who by the
magic of a blue fairy did not need strings anymore? Maybe, as believers in the Lord Jesus Christ,
we shouldn't rely on fairy tales. But, dear child, there
is a lesson for us here.

When Pinocchio still had strings, Geppetto, his
father who created him, controlled his movements and
his very being. When Pinocchio was free, he sang for an
audience, "I got no strings," and proceeded to fall flat
on his face! Later on, he got into all kinds of trouble.

You see, he wished to do "his own thing," but he
needed the strings, the constraints, offered by his
maker. We, too, need constraints. We need to be in
him. For it is only in him that we move freely and are
able to enjoy our very being.

Now, especially in your time of adjustment to a
new manner of living, look to your Maker who
wants you to have your entire being in him.

Prayer focus for today: Those who must work in hazardous situations.

"Do not be afraid. Stand firm and you will see the deliverance the LORD *will bring you today."* (Exodus 14:13)

The Lord tells me not to be afraid. That's so easy to say! I *am* afraid of the future. I'm not sure how I will be able to cope with all the details I have to take care of. How will I be able to stand the loneliness? In reality, then, I am doubting the Lord.

He understands these feelings. He tells us in his word not to be afraid. He does not even want us to waver, doubt, or fear.

His remedy for fear is for us to stand firm. We need to stand firm on his promises. We are called to believe him fully without reservation. When we do so, he promises to deliver us.

He *will* deliver or liberate us from our fears. He assures us that when we claim it, we will find that he has loosened us from the bondage of sorrow and mourning.

Prayer focus for today: Mothers of middle school children.

APRIL 11

And we rejoice in the hope of the glory of God.
(Romans 5:2)

The hymn "Whispering Hope" says, "making my heart in its sorrow rejoice." We're told here to rejoice. Easy for you to say; what do I have to rejoice about? Look further into the Bible verse for today. "The hope of the glory of the God." Why don't I feel hopeful?

Think again of the hymn "Whispering Hope." Does hope come crashing over us like an ocean wave so we cannot help but recognize it? No, my dear child of God, hope whispers to us. It comes to us silently.

That means we need to be still and listen for that gentle whisper, "Hope. Hope. Hope." If you feel there's no future, hear the whisper, "Hope."

If you think you'll never get over this bereavement, hear the whisper, "Hope."

And then think of a phrase from the hymn, "making my heart in its sorrow rejoice."

Wait, listen for the whispered assurance and rejoice.

Prayer focus for today: Reconciliation for estranged families.

APRIL 12

O Lord, do not forsake me; be not far from me, O my God. Come quickly to help me, O Lord my savior. (Psalm 38:21–22)

It is said that when we feel God is far away, he was not the one who moved. He is the same yesterday, today, and tomorrow. We are the ones who moved away from him.

Maybe we say, "Lord, I'm weeping. Don't you know or care? And you assure me that you're right here beside me. You always have been. You always will be.

"So, when I ask you to come quickly to help me, your reply is the same: 'I've always been with you, my dear child. I have never moved from you.'

"When I call to you to be my Savior, your assurance is the same. You're here and ready to protect me."

Hallelujah!

Prayer focus for today: Those who are tempted to falsify their tax returns.

APRIL 13

With the Lord a day is like a thousand years, and a thousand years are like a day. (2 Peter 3:8)

It's been said that we need to be careful about praying for patience. We might be thrust into a situation where patience is essential. Losing our spouses is one of those kinds of situations.

We need patience as we learn to live in a new state of singleness. We need patience with the answers the Lord will send as we ask for assurance. We need patience with ourselves as we struggle to get on with our lives.

We may be days, months, or years into the process of bereavement, and we lament, "Will we ever get over this?" Why do we expect that a day's time will be sufficient for us to learn to adjust to a totally new way of life?

The Lord tells us that to him a day is like a thousand years. His timing and ours are quite different matters. Patience is the watchword for the day or for whatever time it takes.

Praise him for his timing which is perfect!

Prayer focus for today: Those confined to wheelchairs.

"Because he loves me," says the LORD *. . . "I will protect him, for he acknowledges my name." (*Psalm 91:14)

I read those words and I say as a petulant child, "But I do love you, Lord. I always have. Why, then, didn't you protect me from this tragedy in my life?" From my human perspective, I assume that he wanted me to suffer like this.

I go to him and ask him to help me think it through. His answer is that he yearns to protect me. He loved me so much that he sent his only Son to die on a cross to atone for all my sins, to save me. This is superlative protection.

I ask him to forgive me for acting like a child. He surely didn't wish to leave me alone in the world. It's not his choice that I grieve.

But he does promise to protect me where I am. All he asks is that I love him and call on his name.

Prayer focus for today: Christian colleges and universities.

APRIL 15

The LORD does not let the righteous go hungry.
(Proverbs 10:3)

Today is the day that strikes terror in the hearts of many U.S. citizens. It's income tax day, when we must file and possibly pay. Even if we are due a refund, we probably feel that the taxes are too high. We grumble and moan that we won't have enough left to live on.

Look at the words from Proverbs. The Lord assures us that he will not let his righteous go hungry. He will take care of all our needs despite what the government opts to take out of our income.

So, when our paychecks are less than we thought because of a tax increase, we need to remember his promise to his righteous. When our property taxes are higher than we had planned, we need to repeat to ourselves that he will not let his righteous go hungry. When we face higher taxes because we're now filing as a single taxpayer, remember his promise to his righteous children.

Thank you, Lord, for caring so much for me in spite of what we're asked to render unto Caesar.

Prayer focus for today: That we render unto the government fair taxes and to God what he is due.

APRIL 16

Therefore be clear minded and self-controlled so that you can pray. (1 Peter 4:7)

Don't you just love those salad/buffet/dessert bars? There are so many choices. You are certain to find just what you like and lots of it. So you eat, and eat, and you know the rest.

We're told to be clear minded and self-controlled. Boy, is that conviction or what? What's the solution? We have to teach ourselves to make proper choices. We have to learn to partake of proper amounts of the food that's set so temptingly before us.

We need to make proper choices in our adjusting to our new single lives, too. It seems easy to reach out and grab at relationships or practices that may not be healthy for us. It's tempting to overdo and be immersed in our feeling sorry for ourselves.

In all things in our lives, we are called to be clear minded, to be self-controlled, and to pray.

Prayer focus for today: The blind.

APRIL 17

Be transformed by the renewing of your mind.
(Romans 12:2)

Once upon a time, there was a little fuzzy caterpillar. He was happy as he munched green leaves.
It was an idyllic way of living.

One day, he found himself wrapping his body
inside silky threads. What was happening to him? He
had thought he was doing well as a fuzzy caterpillar.
What was this new stage?

He found himself in new surroundings, a chrysalis. It felt very strange. He had trouble adjusting to
it. In many ways, it felt like a prison.

In time, he found himself pushing out at the sides
of the chrysalis. Slowly, he inched himself from the
confines of the chrysalis and into the outside world.
When he was fully out, he realized that instead of being a fuzzy caterpillar, he was now a glorious multi-
colored butterfly. How did that happen? He was
transformed.

If you feel like you're in a chrysalis of your circumstances, remember the caterpillar. He didn't understand either why or who he was, but the transforma-
tion did happen, and the change was beautiful.

Wait and look for how the Lord plans to change
you.

Prayer focus for today: Those facing surgery.

Praise and exalt and glorify the King of heaven, because everything he does is right and all his ways are just. (Daniel 4:37)

When we're in the quicksand of sorrow, we probably don't feel like praising, exalting or glorifying God. We look only downward and see the foundations of our life as we knew it being swallowed up in the mire.

That's the problem. We're looking *downward* to what *was.* Instead, we should try to look *around* us at what *is.* When we can absorb that, we are ready to look up to the King of heaven. When we look up to him, we are more ready to give him proper praise, exaltation, and glorification.

Sometimes, as we look around us at what is, we may question what the Lord chose to do in our lives. Why did he choose death instead of healing? Why didn't he allow rising from the dead? Why? Why? Why?

The answer is that everything he does is right and just. This means everything, whether we like it or understand it. All we're asked to do is continue to give him the honor he is due and praise him for whatever he has done in our lives.

Prayer focus for today: Christian school curricula.

APRIL 19

*When you send your Spirit, they are created, and you
renew the face of the earth.* (Psalm 104:30)

The Lord sends his Holy Spirit to us as a coun-
selor and comforter. Especially now in this hour of
grieving, the Spirit is there beside us, weeping with us
and drying our tears. It is not his desire that we are in
sorrow, but he is more than able to share the burden
with us.

As he sends this Spirit, he promises to renew the
face of the earth. He knows how much we need renewal. Remember, renewal means being made new again.

Once, we did have that ecstatic joy of knowing the
Lord and being born-again. But the experiences of life
have jaded that excitement. Now, at this time of loss,
we find we need to restore our joy of knowing him.

His Spirit is there to help us re-kindle that flame
of knowing the Lord. He will re-new us. All we have
to do is allow him to do this.

Prayer focus for today: Those who are fed at soup kitchens.

"Let light shine out of darkness." (2 Corinthians 4:6)

You surely have heard how much better it is to light one little candle than to complain about the darkness. Are you living right now in a state of being without light, without joy, or without positive hope for your future? Then you might say you're living in darkness.

You know the solution. Light one small candle. Maybe that small candle can be deciding right now that you will begin to make plans for your future. It might mean you consider a change of location or work status. It might be as simple as determining right now that you will search out an alternative pastime you never thought of before.

When you've taken the first step and lit that one small candle, you'll be ready to light more candles and make more concrete plans for what you will do from now on. Before you know it, the light will be sufficient, and you will say, "Thank you, Lord, for bringing so much brightness into my life."

Prayer focus for today: That the terminally ill have assurance of their salvation.

APRIL 21

> *"But whoever listens to me will live in safety."*
> (Proverbs 1:33)

The home security system business is booming. As the prince of this world escalates his attacks on the saints of the Lord, our environments become more and more hazardous.

There's nothing intrinsically wrong with having a security system. But it is my understanding that the professional thieves know how to outwit even the most sophisticated alarm system. It does give you a lot to think about!

So you still decide to install a security system. But are you safe? Think about it. True, lasting safety can only be found in Jesus Christ. No matter what outside threats, thieves, or dangers there are, Jesus alone guarantees total peace and security.

Even now while you're getting used to being widowed, Jesus reaches out to you to offer safety. He offers deliverance from anything in the real or spirit world that threatens to rob you of your security.

Trust in Jesus, the only infallible security system.

Prayer focus for today: Incarcerated persons.

The LORD is God, and he has made his light shine.
(Psalm 118:27)

What happens when your area has an electric power outage? Appliances stop working. The heating/cooling system is non-functional. The lights go out. If it happens after sunset, you are in the dark.

And what happens when you're in the dark? You totter around, probably stubbing your toe on a chair that's familiar because you just couldn't see it. Your environment takes on an eerie appearance. It can be a little scary.

In due time, the problem is resolved and the power is restored. The appliances start to click on again. You have your heating/cooling system back. Best of all, the lights work!

At that moment, you really appreciate those lights. A second before, you were in darkness, and now it is light. Gratitude! Appreciation!

Think about the time you first knew who Jesus is. Your life was in figurative darkness before then. When he became real to you, his light shone down upon you. Surely that light of Jesus was appreciated at that time more because of the darkness where you had been.

Your life today may seem shadow-like in a semi-outage of power. But when you rise above this and see his beaming face, you will be filled with gratitude and appreciation. Wait for it!

Prayer focus for today: Students studying abroad.

APRIL 23

Listen to my prayer, O God, do not ignore my plea; hear me and answer me. My thoughts trouble me and I am distraught. (Psalm 55:1–2)

I once saw a coffee mug with the saying, "It's always darkest before it becomes pitch black!" I thought it was funny at the time. Today as I find myself in the rut of bereavement, I think that saying contains an element of truth. I am troubled. Maybe the darkness of my life is a permanent state.

Now, as I look back over the precious sentences in Psalm 55, I see the word "thoughts" and consider maybe it's my thoughts that are troubling me. The psalmist tells us that our thoughts make us distraught.

But, we're also told in his word that God listens to our pleas. If we ask him to take over our thoughts, he surely will turn them from darkness into light.

Instead of assuming that pitch black is next, let us assume he will answer and that his answer is to blot out all those troubling thoughts. He will bring us into his pure light.

Prayer focus for today: Those in excessive debt.

APRIL 24

I urge you to live a life worthy of the calling you have received. (Ephesians 4:1)

As Christians, we are called to be examples of Christ in the world. That's an awesome responsibility, even when things are going well for us. It's an overwhelming responsibility for us when things are going less than well, like now, when we're still mourning over our loss.

Yet, we're urged to live a life worthy of Christ's calling. How in the world can we do this at this time? The answer is that in the world we can't! You see, when we focus on the world, we are powerless. But when we focus on the One who has called us, we are symbolically lifted out of the constraints of the world. We are endowed with the supernatural power of the Holy Spirit so we can be examples of Christ.

Now, especially in our time of grief, it is vital that we focus on the One and invite his Holy Spirit to lift us up higher and higher. His joy will fill us and the world will marvel to see Christ in us.

Prayer focus for today: Blessings on those who try to walk daily with the Lord.

APRIL 25

Summon your power, O God; show us your strength,
O God, as you have done before. (Psalm 68:28)

L ord, you have done mighty deeds. You formed the
earth, sky, and universe. You set everything in its
proper place. You created us in your image. Your intellect and your strength are unfathomable.

I know you have done mighty deeds. I accept that.
But, Lord, why couldn't you have shown your power
and healed my spouse? Why did you choose to do what
you did?

Nevertheless, I nod my head and bow to you, Lord,
with gratitude for what you did. In my mortal mind,
I don't like it, but in my spiritual mind, I know you
are right.

Thank you, Lord, for showing your power and
might in the way you chose.

Prayer focus for today: Babies born to mothers with
addictions.

A cheerful look brings joy to the heart, and good news gives health to the bones. (Proverbs 15:30)

Psychologists try to get their clients to think positive thoughts. In their secular expertise, they extol the virtues of this. But when you look back into Proverbs, you see that this is not a twentieth-century revelation after all. We're reminded in this verse of the benefits of not thinking negative thoughts.

Can we really do this in our days of mourning? If our hearts are heavy, we're told to put on a cheerful look. How can we do this?

When the tears well up in your eyes, praise the Lord. Praising him brings joy to your soul. You'll soon feel a cheerful look coming. When the negatives of your situation threaten to overtake you, shake your head, rebuke them in the name of Jesus. He will restore your joy. When you feel bone tired because of the physical aspects of being left single, stand up and lift your hands to praise your Abba Father.

He's waiting, gently but assuredly to help you think positively!

Prayer focus for today: Sanitation workers.

APRIL 27

Let the morning bring me word of your unfailing love, for I have put my trust in you. (Psalm 143:8)

Are you in the evening or the nighttime of your grieving? Alone with your sadness, the bed seems so lonely and the nights so long. Will they ever end? Will you always feel like this?

Look at the words of the psalmist. There is the word you're looking for. The griefs, the sadness, the pain, the loneliness may be upon you, but His word, His assurance of unfailing love comes glowing through the windows. At first, it's gentle like the first rays of dawn. It gradually builds until the sunlight splashes into the room and fills it with His glory.

His glory will surround you because, as the psalmist reminds you: put your trust in God. When you trust, truly trust God, he will give you assurances of his unfailing love.

Praise the great God who never fails!

Prayer focus for today: Reconciliation between ethnic groups.

APRIL 28

"Therefore I tell you, do not worry about your life, what you will eat or drink; or about your body, what you will wear." (Matthew 6:25)

"But, Lord, you just don't know. The bills are inundating me. My grocery budget is beyond me. What will I wear? But, Lord . . ."

And then he says, "You're worrying again."

Worrying means we don't really trust the Lord. We think he will let us down. He doesn't care or understand.

How audacious of us to worry. Jesus himself tells us not to worry.

"But, Lord . . ."

And he reiterates, "Do not worry. It was I who created you and I do care. It's all under control. All your worrying is unnecessary."

So, close your eyes, crawl up into his lap and bask in his love. Let him stroke your head gently. Trust him and say:

"Lord! Lord!"

Prayer focus for today: Parents of children who are out of control.

APRIL 29

Unless the LORD *watches over the city, the watchmen stand guard in vain.* (Psalm 127:1)

When stopping at a rest area on an interstate highway, I'm always relieved to see twenty-four-hour security. Just the sight of uniformed, armed police officers makes me feel safe. I'm especially sensitive to this now that, as a woman by myself, I drive many places alone.

But then I think about it and realize what this verse is telling me. It's prudent to look for secure rest stops. But my safety doesn't really depend on a uniformed, armed police officer. My security is assured by the presence of the Almighty God.

When I am in the car alone, I'm not really alone. His angels form a hedge of protection around my vehicle. My Abba Father is riding right there with me. He alone is watching over me. He alone is more than sufficient to keep me safe.

Thank you, Lord.

Prayer focus for today: Blessings on the meek.

I cried out to God for help; I cried out to God to hear me. When I was in distress, I sought the Lord. (Psalm 77:1–2)

Does this verse hit you in the pit of your stomach? It does me. I cry to the Lord for help. I cry for him to hear me. I really am in communication with him now in my bereavement. I'm in distress. I seek him.

Why don't I talk to him as much when I'm not in distress? How come it takes overwhelming tragedy for me to seek his face and talk, really talk to him?

Is it because I secretly think I can handle life just fine by myself when things are going well? Do I feel I don't need his help when the way is smooth? Do I just refuse to acknowledge his Lordship at all times of my life?

The beauty of all this is that he is there waiting. He waits while I am blissfully ignoring him in the good times. And he's willing to subject me to tremendous stress to show me how to appreciate his Lordship.

Prayer focus for today: Directors of Christian education.

MAY 1

The garment of praise for the spirit of heaviness.
(Isaiah 61:3 KJV)

When I think of the garment of praise, I picture a long, white, flowing robe. It is soft to the touch and gentle on the skin. It has a delightfully pleasant aroma. It would feel so good to be clothed in this robe. Snuggled in this garment of praise, I would feel so safe. All I do is praise the Lord while I am covered with his robe.

The Lord Jesus Christ is also a covering for us. He promises to those of us who are born-again that he will cover us with his blood. But you may say, "Blood is red. That covering would be red."

What else is red, dear child? Our sins are red, scarlet red. Now, picture this. Our sins are as scarlet. The Lord Jesus Christ covers us with his blood, also red. If you look at red through a transparent substance that's red, the result is pure, clear white.

Our Lord Jesus Christ covers our scarlet sins with his very own shed blood. When the Father looks at us through his Son's precious blood, he sees us only as pure.

Praise God! How dare I have a spirit of heaviness? No sorrow of this world can rob me of the utter joy of knowing that the God of the universe covers me totally, completely, purely.

Prayer focus for today: Parents who must work several jobs.

MAY 2

"Come, let us rebuild the wall of Jerusalem, and we will no longer be in disgrace." (Nehemiah 2:17)

In the part of country where I once lived, brick homes and buildings are prevalent. There are bricks of very red tones, of coral or pink, and even variegated bricks. You see differing patterns of the ways bricks are laid. It's fun to watch the bricklayers as they create their patterns by building one upon another and another.

It must have been exciting to see the walls of Jerusalem being rebuilt. These walls had been broken down and burned by enemies of Israel. At first Nehemiah might have said, "What a mess. What a lot of ruins!" But, slowly, consistently, stone by stone he oversaw the walls and various gates being restored once again. Out of the rubble, a substantial wall was built.

Do you feel your life is a rubble of broken down ruins of what once was or might have been? Has the enemy, death, broken down your wall of protection?

Take a lesson from Nehemiah and begin to rebuild your life, slowly, consistently, brick by brick.

You can do it!

Prayer focus for today: Emergency Medical Personnel.

MAY 3

But if we walk in the light, as he is in the light, we have fellowship with one another. (1 John 1:7)

One definition of walking in the light can be walking as you shine a lamp on the path ahead of you. Think about what that means. Does the lamp illuminate the whole path for miles ahead? Can you see for miles ahead? No, dear child of God, all you see for certain is the path that is lit by the beacon. Your task is to walk in the light that you do see and trust what lies ahead.

Your life can be like walking in the lamp-lit path. Today you may feel the future is bleak and indiscernible. All you're expected to do is put one foot in front of the other in the light of what you do see and are sure of.

It's all right to think about the future and try to plan ahead for your now single life. But take steps toward your plans one at a time.

Let the Light of Jesus be the lamp for your feet and trust where and how far he wants you to go.

Prayer focus for today: That believers seek the Kingdom of God first.

"May you be richly rewarded by the LORD, the God of Israel, under whose wings you have come to take refuge." (Ruth 2:12)

Is there anything more appealing or helpless than a baby chick? The little creature is soft and fragile. It looks around wide-eyed and naive. The only noises it makes are faint little peeps.

The Creator who made all things was aware of the little one's frailty. So he provided the mother hen to protect and safeguard the baby chick. Under the wings of the mother hen, it is safe. Under her nurturing, it grows until it is strong enough to go out into the world.

Our Father God is ready to protect you in much the same way. Maybe today in your sorrow you feel vulnerable and weak as the baby chick. That's OK. Be gentle with yourself. You've been through a traumatic experience. It's OK to feel fragile.

Rest under the wings of your Father God. He is there to protect and nurture you. In time, you will feel stronger and be ready to go out into your world. When you do, keep returning to him as your protector.

Prayer focus for today: Parents who have lost a child to leukemia.

MAY 5

> *"For the eyes of the* LORD *range throughout the earth to strengthen those whose hearts are fully committed to him."* (2 Chronicles 16:9)

What do you picture when you think of the eyes of the Lord searching the entire world to find those who are committed to him? These words can stimulate your imagination in a multitude of ways.

I think of the Lord as a bright, unimaginably, brilliant light. Beams radiate from this light like searchlights over the world as he looks for those who claim him as Savior. These beams project great distances. They permeate around and into every nook and cranny of our earth. Nothing is hidden from his penetrating light.

When he finds one of his own, he showers his light upon that one. The search light of the Lord recognizes everything about his own. He knows our joys. He knows our sorrows. He knows our hopes. He knows our secrets. He knows our guilt. But his knowing all about us is not a condemnation. It is to strengthen us who are fully committed to him.

So, rejoice when his searchlight finds you and shines on you. It is another affirmation of his deep love and concern for all areas of your life.

Prayer focus for today: Specific people in your life who need salvation.

MAY 6

For the LORD *will go before you, the God of Israel will be your rear guard.* (Isaiah 52:12)

When your spouse died, did you feel all alone? Do you still feel that you just can't go on alone? Well, dear child of God, the good news is that you don't have to. Our God, the Mighty One of Israel, is right there with you.

He has promised that he will go before you. He will lead the way for you. With his power, he'll break any barriers that threaten to stop you, his own dear child. He will fight the battle for you. All you have to do is continue to walk the path he has blazed for you.

But you say, "What about those dangers that sneak up behind and threaten to ambush me?" Dear child, he has promised that he will be your rear guard. Not only is he running interference for you, but he is following, alertly watching out for any remnants of danger.

Rest in the total security that Christ indeed is before you, beside you, behind you, surrounding you with his almighty protection.

Prayer focus for today: Those who sponsor Bible Clubs for children.

MAY 7

I will exalt you, O LORD, for you lifted me out of the depths. (Psalm 30:1)

There's a lot to learn from observing people on escalators. They step on and just stand there. They don't have to do a thing and they are elevated. Many don't even watch where they're going and seem almost surprised when they reach the top.

My favorite type of escalators are those that take you up from a subway station. You step on the escalator while you're still underground. You're not doing anything or even thinking about it, but you're being lifted upward. Soon you find yourself in the bright, sunlit, outside world.

Do you see yourself in this picture? Is the subway a symbol of where you are in the depths of your bereavement? The Lord wants to lift you up out of those depths and into his "Sonlight."

All you have to do is be willing to step onto his escalator.

Prayer focus for today: Mothers of high school children.

MAY 8

"Who of you by worrying can add a single hour to his life?" (Matthew 6:27)

Are yo-yo's a toy for children? Or are they for adults? I've seen kids really frustrated tying to make a yo-yo merely do its up and down motion. Then I've seen adults (mostly on television) who make the yo-yo do all sorts of strange contortions, rocking, almost standing still, doing loop-de-loops. It's enough to boggle the mind.

Whatever intricate motions the yo-yo expert puts it through, the basic motion of a yo-yo is still up and down, up and down. It doesn't really go anywhere.

Worrying is a lot like the yo-yo. You can dress it up and call it concern. You can fret about your burdens, but worry is still worry, and it doesn't get you anywhere. Some days a lot, some days a little, still up and down, nowhere.

Is there a solution? Of course there is, dear child of God. Look at who asks the question about worrying: our Lord Jesus Christ, the one who knows you and loves you. He knows that worry about your finances, about your widowhood, and about your grief will only be a yo-yo.

Trust him and throw that yo-yo away!

Prayer focus for today: Christian magazines.

MAY 9

> *Your love, O LORD, reaches to the heavens, your faith-*
> *fulness to the skies.* (Psalm 36:5)

A child asks, "How big is God?" We may stammer and sputter some answer about God being spirit. The child is puzzled. The size of God is a mystery to the child. Maybe it's a mystery to us as well.

We read that his love reaches to the heavens. That's pretty big! How does he do this? We enlightened adults don't know either. Our God is so magnificent that we can't even begin to fathom it while we're in the flesh. We'll have to wait until we enter Glory to comprehend and truly worship our great God.

In the meantime, he's given us word pictures and visual demonstrations so we can catch a glimmer of him. When I look up at the skies and the clouds, I often think, "God sees those clouds from the other side!" The night my husband died, there was a thunderstorm. One of my friends noted, "This is the first time Earl's seen this from the other side."

When I think of the skies, the heavens as we see them in that light, I am comforted. May you look upward to the heavens and feel his peace.

Prayer focus for today: Seminary students.

In his heart a man plans his course, but the LORD determines his steps. (Proverbs 16:9)

Experts write books, appear on TV talk shows, and inundate magazines with how-to's on planning your life. We say, "I'll be across the city in twenty minutes," and make our plans accordingly. And then we come across a major traffic tie-up that delays us for an additional thirty minutes. We have planned our course, but the Lord determines our steps.

Maybe you and your spouse had planned to take a trip to Europe, tour Hawaii, travel around the world in eighty days. You planned your course together.

And then what happened? Your steps were determined by the Lord. He said, "Your plans are changed. Your spouse is now not part of those plans. You must take different steps."

Just know that the Perfect Planner is in charge of your life. He knows what you have hoped for in this life, but he also knows the perfect ending to the story!

Prayer focus for today: Those who need to pause and reflect on God's goodness.

MAY 11

Find out what pleases the Lord. (Ephesians 5:10)

I entered the restaurant. It was elegant. The maitre d' said, "Only one?" I ignored the comment and said, "One." He placed me at a lovely table set for two. There I was seated across a candlelit table staring at an empty chair. It was a beautiful chair, carved wood, padded back, but it was still empty.

As I sat there, I remembered another single, very elegant lady, whose standard response to the raised eyebrow question of, "Only one?" is "No, Jesus is here with me."

And then it hit me! That chair across from me was not empty. Jesus was there with me. What a precious, intimate moment this could be. Jesus, my beloved Savior, was sitting there desiring to spend time alone just with me!

It was a perfect time to talk with him and to ask what he would like me to do. It was an opportunity to find out what pleases him. It was a moment I will cherish for the rest of my life.

Prayer focus for today: Those who are in physical danger.

But I will sing of your strength, in the morning I will sing of your love; for you are my fortress, my refuge in times of trouble. (Psalm 59:16)

Little children love to sing. They hear a tune on the radio, they listen to their teacher, and they sing, off key or on key. They sing their little hearts out. The song may not always come out the way they heard it. For example, my four-year-old granddaughter sang, with heart-felt emotion, "We wish you a Merry Christmas and a happy two ears."

We may be amused by little children and their musical renditions, but the important point is that they are willing to sing, make mistakes, and try again. What happens to us as we become mature adults? Do we risk being heard as we sing on or off key, wrong or right words?

Our Lord inhabits the praises and singing of his people. Do we assign the chore of singing only to little children? Why don't we stiff adults also enter in completely singing his praises?

The psalmist sang to his Lord. Just imagine the pleasure our Lord took in hearing the psalmist sing to him. Imagine the pleasure he takes when we sing to him as well.

Prayer focus for today: Those who feel their lives are useless.

MAY 13

Be imitators of God, therefore, as dearly loved children. (Ephesians 5:1)

Have you had any experience with liturgical clowning? Generally when people think of clowns, they laugh. In clowning, the actions are imitations of real people and are done in such a way that the clown appears to be a fool. In liturgical clowning, the mime or clown strives to be a fool for Christ.

The preparation time to become a liturgical clown can be extensive. Prayer is always part of before, during, and after performances. Covering the face with white grease paint is symbolic of dying to self for the sake of the Lord. While in white face, the clown traditionally is silent. Even while applying the make-up, he is silent. Colors are added to the white face as symbols of new life we all have in Jesus. Most liturgical clowns add a red dot to one cheek symbolizing the love kiss from Jesus.

In many liturgical clown skits, there is a Christ figure. This person stands out and is frequently marked with red dots on the palms for the nailprints and/or a cross on the attire or make-up. All the clowns, however, have the honor of being imitators of Christ as they perform.

Maybe today, in your mind's eye, you will see yourself putting on white to symbolize dying to self and then applying the first new colors of new life in him as you look ahead to what he's planned for you from now on.

Prayer focus for today: Those who face a job change.

Answer me, O LORD, out of the goodness of your love;
in your good mercy turn to me. (Psalm 69:16)

L ord, I really needed answers when you took my
spouse away. I still don't understand fully why,
when there was so much more living we had to do
together. All of us gathered there in the emergency
room prayed fervently for you to heal him. Didn't
you hear us, Lord?

The doctors were puzzled about his high fever.
Where did he get this infection? What specifically was
it? They paced the floor as they, too, needed answers.

The nurses carried out their assignments while
they were dazed to see such a strong virile man so ill.
They, too, asked for answers. When his heart stopped,
one of them had to be the one to tell me what had
happened and that the doctors were trying CPR.

I remember sitting there feeling a gentle breeze
flow across my face. I remember saying, "He just
can't die."

I now know that the breeze was his spirit coming
to say "Goodbye" before you, Lord, escorted him
into Glory. And I also know that you, Lord, gave me
an answer by allowing his spirit to bid me farewell.

May this day be one for you when you recognize
the answers he gives to you.

Prayer focus for today: Peacemakers.

MAY 15

We are hard pressed on every side, but not crushed.
(2 Corinthians 4:8)

At their wedding, my son and daughter-in-law gave me a beautiful long-stemmed, red rose. I enjoyed it at the reception and then gently carried it with me on the airplane trip home. My desire was to preserve it in the best way I knew.

Tenderly, I put it between layers of paper towels. I arranged the rose to look its best and then placed it inside a large book, weighing it down with still more large books. After several weeks, I looked inside to see it. There it was, pressed and still all in one piece.

Our lives can be like that pressed rose. In our bereavement, we may feel hard pressed, squeezed, or caught under the weight of our grief. But just as that rose was not crushed because it was protected by those soft layers of paper towels, we too can stand being hard pressed. We know that our Lord Jesus Christ is there protecting us and keeping us from shattering.

Through all of this, we can emerge intact, changed surely, but secure in him.

Prayer focus for today: Those who have difficulty walking.

MAY 16

"I have come that they may have life, and have it to the full." (John 10:10)

Nothing is the same, Lord. I'll never enjoy life again. I really miss my spouse. Is life as I knew it over for me?

No, your life isn't over, though some experiences or situations you shared with your spouse are no more. But that doesn't mean it's the end of everything.

Maybe God is calling you to change direction, career, or location. He is eager for you to thrive in the life you have now. He made you and, as your Abba Father, he wants you to have life to the full.

His choice is to come to you and give you the abundant life. Your task is to come to him, listen to what he has to say to you, and receive the fullness of joy he has waiting for you.

Prayer focus for today: High-risk pregnancies.

MAY 17

The man of integrity walks securely. (Proverbs 10:9)

I am a walker. My pattern has been to walk forty-five minutes early in the morning and about thirty minutes in the evening. When I started walking, I thought any kind of tennis shoes would do. Was I ever wrong! I soon learned I needed to go to one of those stores that specializes in athletic shoes.

Have you looked at the varieties of athletic shoes that are available today? Even a quick glance at the store windows reveals shoes for aerobics, for cross-training, for running, high tops, low tops. It's enough to confuse anyone!

I found the shoes for walking. A few days of using my appropriate shoes made me realize the value of ones that are made just for this activity. Exercising is much easier now.

But, you know, there's a class of walking that doesn't require the proper shoes in earthly terms. The Scriptures tell us a "man of integrity walks securely." When we let ourselves walk with the Lord daily, no matter what the circumstances, we have perfect peace. The only preparation we need for this walk is to be born-again.

Keep on walking!

Prayer focus for today: Those who have been injured in car accidents.

Help us, O God our Savior, for the glory of your name.
(Psalm 79:9)

These days there's a glut of television and radio programs on marriage. You'll find topics on how to better your marriage, your family life, and your sex life. There's nothing wrong with these articles and other presentations. They're undoubtedly needed in the light of the skyrocketing rate of divorce in our country. But, when you've just been widowed, those programs can be painful reminders of what once was.

I get agitated when a television or radio show comes on with "experts" telling us how to make our marriage complete. How can it be "complete" when there's only one of me? I change the channel, and search for a program on anything else. Frequently, I just turn it off and go to my room to spend time alone with my Lord.

My Lord has promised to help us. To me that means he cares. When I am agitated about the reminders of a lost love, he assures me that those feelings are OK. I cry if I must. Then I wash my face, dry my tears, and go out to face the next day of adjusting to my singleness.

And he goes out there with me, my God, my Savior, my helper.

Prayer focus for today: Public school curricula.

MAY 19

"This man is my chosen instrument." (Acts 9:15)

S aul of Tarsus probably was voted "most likely to succeed." He had everything going for him. He was bright and educated—the Hebrew of the Hebrews. He was such a good company man that he was a leader of the pack who persecuted the early Christians.

Then God in his infinite understanding of Saul put him in a situation where conversion to the true faith in Jesus was the only answer. "Saul" became "Paul." Using Paul's intellect and writing skills, God has communicated to all Christians since then. Paul was truly the Lord's chosen instrument.

We humans may look at the first part of the story and judge Saul to be a most unlikely person to be part of the Christian church, but God knew the potential and the end of the story.

He knows your potential, too. You may ask, "Why did he put me into this single situation? I didn't have a vote in this!"

Remember Saul who became Paul—chosen by God. You are indeed chosen by God to be in this situation at this time. Look for what he's telling you and seek to be the best for him.

Prayer focus for today: Families of pastors.

"Knowledge of the Holy One is understanding."
(Proverbs 9:10)

It was the first night of the adult education courses at the local high school. I had enrolled by mail into the beginning Spanish course. The first night, I planned to arrive on the high school campus near the starting time of the first session. I pulled into the parking lot. It was big, but it was full of cars. They were everywhere, in staff-only spaces, on the grass, and out on the street. I drove my car up and down, much as a shark, circling for a legal place to park my car. Finally I found a place!

As I walked through the sea of parked cars, I was impressed by the numbers of people who enrolled in adult education courses. That was good. We surely don't know it all. There's lots of knowledge to be gained.

I remembered these words from Proverbs. What knowledge is most important? It's fine to learn more about life while we're in the flesh. But only the knowledge of the Holy One is lasting for all eternity. Only the knowledge of the Holy One is where our comfort comes. Only the knowledge of the Holy One brings joy that will be endless.

Praise him!

Prayer focus for today: Leaders of groups who minister to teenagers.

MAY 21

O LORD, you have searched me and you know me.
(Psalm 139:1)

When I think of the Lord searching and knowing me, I think of a microscope. Picture it! The Lord who created me knows every little detail about my being. He doesn't need some sort of "cosmic microscope" to be able to see everything about me. He knows because he knows!

There are times when I wish we could use microscopes to figure out what's going on. For example, my second son is a diagnosed schizophrenic. Over the years, I've read what is available on the subject. Today's assumption seems to be that it is caused by a chemical imbalance, but this can't be determined specifically for each of the persons who suffer from it. Oh, if there were only a way to use a microscope to look more closely at the way a given schizophrenic's body is constructed, there might be a way to correct the condition.

But we can't do that. Only the Lord knows the situation. He knows my son. He sees him with his microscope. He knows the prayers that have been offered on my son's behalf. It is the Lord's choice to remain still and let this disability continue.

In this heartache, and in the heartache of widowhood, my only contentment can be found in knowing that my Lord truly knows all details and knows what is best.

Prayer focus for today: Students in public schools.

MAY 22

A thousand may fall at your side, ten thousand at
your right hand, but it will not come near you.
(Psalm 91:7)

If you are into statistics, you may know that there
are 13.9 million widowed persons in the United
States. That's a lot of people who are going through
what you are going through.

How do you suppose all of them are coping with
their status of singlehood? They are coping in many
ways, to be sure. Months after the death of their
spouses, some are still sobbing and shaking fists at
God. I've met some of them. You probably have, too.
They can be put in the category of the thousands
who figuratively fall. They haven't fully latched onto
the comfort and pure solace to be found in Christ
Jesus.

Some of those thousands look at me with puz-
zlement. They can't fathom how I could have worn a
pink dress to my husband's funeral, or why I insist-
ed on having praise tapes played before the service
actually began. Any chance I get, I tell them it was a
celebration service.

Those thousands need our prayers.

Prayer focus for today: Dysfunctional families.

MAY 23

We are more than conquerors through him who loved us.
(Romans 8:37)

What's the definition of a conqueror? A victor? A champion? An ace? A possessor of a Congressional Medal of Honor perhaps?

Have you received a Congressional Medal of Honor lately? It doesn't matter at all because we're told we are more than that. The Medal of Honor we have is eternal life. Hallelujah!

We are champions over any darts this earthly life can throw our way. We are victorious over sorrow, fear, and loneliness.

Our task, then, is to reach joyfully to the Lord and let him comfort us by reminding us of our role as more than conquerors.

Prayer focus for today: Those who live in isolated locations.

MAY 24

How many are your works, O Lord! In wisdom you made them all; the earth is full of your creatures. (Psalm 104:24)

You've made a beautiful world, Lord! I marvel daily to see the sun rise and set, to see the majestic oceans, and to watch the tiniest ant colony work together with precision. What a spectacular engineer you are, Lord!

I think of how my own body is made. What a wonder it is to see how you created every system, every fiber of my being. It is more than I can fathom.

If I ponder too much upon myself, I find my thoughts turning inward to my own grief and I begin to feel sorry for myself.

Then you remind me that this is self-defeating. You tell me, "Look instead at the world I made for you."

Thank you, Lord, for reminding me to look outward. I see the iridescent colors of a rainbow. I see a yellow butterfly resting on a fuchsia flower. I hear a chipmunk crunching nuts. I feel your gentle breeze sweep by.

Thank you, Lord, for helping me approach an attitude of thanksgiving and peace in my circumstances.

Prayer focus for today: Make us more faithful in our prayer life.

MAY 25

I pray that out of his glorious riches, he may strengthen you with power through his Spirit in your inner being. (Ephesians 3:16)

There is a young man who is dear to me. At one time, he was employed by a huge corporation whose main source of profit was defense contracts. It was fine until, as he quipped, "Peace broke out."

Within the company there were drastic changes. Layoffs were rampant. Salaries were slashed. Rumors abounded about more and more pink slips. The employees lived day to day with the fear of being terminated. And the economy of the community began to suffer. People took huge losses when they sold their homes.

While this was going on, I was in fervent prayer for this young man and his family. One Sunday morning, the Lord gave me a vision of him. Over his head was a golden door which opened to shower material gifts and money upon him. This was a blessed promise from the Lord that he wanted to shower his glorious riches on this young man.

The end of the story is that my friend has now relocated far from the area where this occurred. He is receiving many of the promised financial blessings which were prophesied.

If the Lord can do this, surely he will bless the widowed as well.

Prayer focus for today: Prison ministries.

For in the day of trouble he will keep me safe in his dwelling; he will hide me in the shelter of his tabernacle and set me high upon a rock. (Psalm 27:5)

Our Lord has promised us that he will keep us safe in his dwelling or in his tabernacle. Have you ever pondered what it would be like to be part of the children of Israel as they wandered around for forty years?

The Lord told Moses to build a place of worship for the Israelites. Since they were nomadic, this worship had to take place in a moveable structure called a tabernacle. He gave Moses specific instructions on how it was to be built and transported. The children of Israel, therefore, had a place where they could follow the mandates of worship as set up by God.

The tabernacle probably was the one place they could feel secure as they wandered in the wilderness. They were in a strange land and lost, not knowing they were really taking a circular route. The tabernacle represented safety wherever they were.

Do you sometimes feel as if you're wandering around in circles in a desert of your life? Has your bereavement left you wondering if you'll ever get anywhere?

Enter the tabernacle or place of worship as speedily as you can. It is there you will find the security he offers so freely.

Prayer focus for today: Family-oriented television shows.

MAY 27

> *"Love the Lord your God with all your heart and with all your soul and with all your mind."*
> (Matthew 22:37)

When we love someone, we want to be with that person no matter what. There's an old story involving a young man who expressed his devotion to his beloved with:

"I'd climb the highest mountain, swim the deepest ocean, cross the barren desert for you. (P.S. I'll be over Saturday night if it doesn't rain.)"

Are we like that in our love for God? Do we love him so much that we're willing to get up an hour early to commune with him? Do we love him enough to give up watching a Sunday football game in order to go to a worship service? Or will we be over Saturday night if it doesn't rain?

As soon as we add "if," we are limiting our love for him. We are called to love him with our heart, soul, and mind. We are called to love him totally with no ifs, just to love him.

Decide now to give him your full heart, soul, and mind, and love him without reservation.

Prayer focus for today: Students participating in adult literacy programs.

*May you be blessed by the L*ORD*, the Maker of heaven and earth.* (Psalm 115:15)

One definition of blessed is "to set something apart for sacred use." We may think of it as shewbread, chalices, or altar paraments when we think of blessed things. But have you ever considered yourself to have been set apart for sacred use?

You may hesitate to consider yourself as a blessing, but think about it, especially now as you're adjusting to your new life of singleness. When you were married, you had to consider everything in the light of being one of two. Now that there's only one of you, try to look at it as a blessing of being set apart for a specific calling from the Lord. This calling is for you alone.

Maybe he wants you to take a ministry you couldn't have thought of before. You're free now to counsel people at odd hours if need be. Short term mission trips may now be possible. He may even be calling you to take Bible courses or prepare for a career in the ministry.

Rejoice and see what his purpose is in setting you apart for sacred use!

Prayer focus for today: Children in day care.

MAY 29

Jesus Christ is the same yesterday and today and forever.
(Hebrews 13:8)

There's one thing in life that we know with certainty: nothing ever stays the same. The clouds in the sky are in a constant state of change. Grass grows. The rose bud becomes a flower and then drops its petals. And we who have lost a spouse to death are painfully aware of how quickly and how overwhelmingly changes happen.

We were married. Now we're not. There were two incomes. Now there's one. We had someone to share our thoughts with. Now we're alone.

But we have the assurance of one thing in this life and beyond. That is Jesus Christ. He is always there. He always has been there. He was there at the creation of the world when God said, "Let us make man in *our* image." He was here in a human body so he could show us the way. He's with the Father in heaven now where he waits to greet us when we join him in eternity.

What a comfort it is to know with absolute certainty that Jesus was, is, and will be our same dependable Savior.

Prayer focus for today: Nurses caring for patients in intensive care units.

My people will live in peaceful dwelling places, in secret homes, in undisturbed places of rest. (Isaiah 32:18)

It's easy to become apprehensive when you're put in a position of living alone. The creaking floor boards seem deafening. The second chair at the kitchen table reminds you that you are alone. The empty closet that once held your spouse's clothes seems to mock you. The nights are so long. The bed is so empty. You ask the Lord, "Where is my place in all of this?"

The Lord promises us that our homes will be peaceful, secure, and restful. Why do you suppose we don't feel that in our hours of sorrow?

Maybe the key is that we are apprehensive because we assume we are living alone. Didn't our Savior tell us that where his servant is, he will be also? So, dear child of God, we are not alone.

When circumstances of apprehension, sown by the Enemy, tell you you're alone, rebuke them in the precious name of Jesus. Claim the peace of knowing Jesus is right there with you

Hallelujah!

Prayer focus for today: Love among Christians.

MAY 31

> *Those who hope in the* LORD *will renew their strength.*
> *They will soar on wings like eagles; they will run and*
> *not grow weary, they will walk and not be faint.*
> (Isaiah 40:31)

Since your spouse died, do you find that you are extremely tired? Do you sometimes feel that your strength is almost gone? Do you feel that you should be able to snap out of it?

Dear child of God, it's OK to feel that way. You've been through an extremely stressful time. Don't be too hard on yourself. Give yourself time to let the balm of Gilead soak into your soul.

When you're ready to think about these words from Isaiah, try to think of the mighty eagle. These words say that we shall be like that eagle. We can soar above all earthly circumstances. It is promised that we will never tire, never grow weary, and will walk and not faint.

Don't expect this all at once. Your body needs time to heal. Your heart needs time to begin to mend its brokenness.

All we have to do is hope in the Lord.

Prayer focus for today: Families of runaways.

JUNE 1

*Instead of the thornbush will grow the pine tree, and
instead of briers the myrtle will grow.* (Isaiah 55:13)

Most people assume that growing Christmas
trees is child's play. You plant those cute little
seedlings in the ground. Then you stand back and
watch them grow into income-producing commodi-
ties. Sounds good, doesn't it?

The reality is that growing Christmas trees is not
easy. There's shearing, mowing, and spraying, to
mention only three of the myriad of things that need
to be done to produce quality trees.

And then there are the big time weeds that grow in
the fields. Kudzu creepingly crawls over everything
so you can't even see where those cute little seedlings
are. Tall grasses fall down and knock the little seedlings over. And worst of all is the multiflora rose
that chokes out even the most stalwart Christmas
tree. It has huge thorns that can tear at your flesh as
you try to remove the rose that's really a weed.

Are there thorny multiflora rose bushes in your
life? You probably accepted that your life was not
going to be child's play, but did you expect so many
thorns and briers?

The good news that the Lord offers us is that the
pine tree and myrtle will grow. Take heart in that,
dear child of God.

Prayer focus for today: Those recovering from surgery.

JUNE 2

> *"For where your treasure is, there your heart will be also."* (Matthew 6:21)

Treasure, by definition, usually refers to items with monetary value. You treasure your bank accounts, your house, your car, and your retirement fund.

When you treasure something, you may also cherish it. Cherish is a word we frequently equate with the love we have for another.

We treasure some*thing*. We cherish some*body*. Our heart is there with that something or somebody. What happens when we lose what has our heart? When we lose somebody, especially a spouse, we run the risk of having our heart broken.

Once the dust clears and we start to put a splint on our broken heart, we need to look up and see the One who is the only real treasure, the One we really should cherish.

Jesus, and Jesus alone, is the One who is the treasure worthy of giving our heart to wholly and completely.

Prayer focus for today: Teachers in Christian schools.

JUNE 3

But he knows the way I take; when he has tested me, I will come forth as gold. (Job 23:10)

Have you ever seen pictures of an experiment with a rat trying to find his way through a maze? The rat runs merrily down one passageway, turns a corner, and finds a dead end. He goes the other way and bangs into a wall. He scurries across another intersection. Surely this is the right way—and you guessed it, it's the end of the line.

This stop-and-start, hit-or-miss performance repeats until the rat finally figures out the correct route through the maze. While all this is going on, scientific observers are watching and taking notes on what the rat has found, how he's coping with the frustration, and how clever he really is.

We can feel like that rat in the maze. We choose one way and are thwarted. We find a path that is comfortable and suddenly it ends. That's a little like our lives have been. Our marriage was a chosen path; suddenly it's over. Like the rat, we may wonder if there's someone watching us taking notes.

Someone is watching us, but he's not taking notes. He's cheering us on. The Lord knows the ways we take. It may seem like a test, but he has unspeakable joy ahead for us. Trust him to carry us through.

Prayer focus for today: Those who are indifferent to the calling of the Lord.

JUNE 4

"If you believe, you will receive whatever you ask for in prayer." (Matthew 21:22)

You told me, Lord, that if I *believe*, I will receive. Well, I believed. I prayed, how I prayed that my spouse would not die. My Christian brothers and sisters were on their knees also. Even after the doctors came and said, "It's over," they continued to pray for a raising from the dead.

I believed. They believed. We all believed. How come we didn't receive?

What is "believe"? To be sure? To be convinced? Job said, "Though he slay me, yet I will hope in him . . . indeed this will turn out for my deliverance" (Job 13:15–16).

Maybe that's the key. Believe no matter what, no matter what happens, no matter if the answer is "no." Just believe.

Prayer focus for today: Choir directors.

JUNE 5

"The glory of this present house will be greater than the glory of the former house." (Haggai 2:9)

In the Old Testament, the glory of the Lord was represented with a cloud that filled the temple. Just imagine the glory of the Lord filling your house as this verse suggests.

You may feel that your house was indeed a Godly one. You and your spouse did your best to use it to show the love of Jesus to others. You had a glimmer of the glory of the Lord within your own four walls.

So now, that part of your life is no more and the former house is gone. Does this mean the glory of the Lord has left also?

Look at this verse again. What does it promise? The Lord is telling you that what is to come will be greater than what was before. What was before is not forgotten. It's part of you, but the new he has promised will be full of his glory. Wait and watch!

Prayer focus for today: Group residences for the mentally ill.

JUNE 6

Your words have supported those who stumbled; you have strengthened faltering knees. But now trouble comes to you, and you are discouraged. (Job 4:4–5)

Lord, I've always had a ministry of being a pillar of faith to others. In groups, people look to me for answers to their questions. Friends call on me to be a listener while they dump their problems on me. Even my own family thinks I am a Bible scholar. I'm just great at solving other people's problems.

But in this today of my life, I am discouraged. The troubles of sorrow and loneliness have come to me. All my bravado and advice are like the chaff the wind blows away. Who was I kidding? I don't really know that much. My faith must not be worth much if I falter now.

And then you calmly assure me that during all those times you were there supporting me. While I was being the authority or advisor, you were there with me, encouraging me and giving me the words to say.

So forgive me, Lord, for being discouraged in this temporary setback in the ministry you called me to.

Prayer focus for today: Legal aliens who have come to our country.

The light shines in the darkness. (John 1:5)

My sorrow absolutely engulfs me. In the inky shadows of this nighttime of my life, I am overcome with my grief. When I am in this darkness, I can see nothing, so there must be nothing left for me.

But, as it is suggested, it's always darkest before the dawn, and so the light of the Lord comes to us. He knows how scary the dark is. He understands the dark is not a preferred mode for us. He also knows how much of this darkness we can tolerate.

Just when we think the darkness, the sorrow, is all we can take, he comes to us and in his infinite wisdom, he lets the dawn break in our lives.

Maybe if the light came too soon, it would blind us because we were so accustomed to the dark. So he waits to bring his light to us at the appropriate time.

Praise God for his perfect timing.

Prayer focus for today: Children who are fatherless.

JUNE 8

Acknowledge and take to heart this day that the LORD is God in heaven above and on the earth below. There is no other. (Deuteronomy 4:39)

The seven-year-old asks, "Where is God?" What is the answer? This verse explains that the Lord is in heaven above and on the earth below. In other words, he is omnipresent. He is everywhere. If the seven-year-old doesn't understand that, it's OK. I don't know many adults who truly understand either. The Lord said it, and that should be good enough for anybody.

He also tells us that not only is he present in heaven and on earth, but he is Lord of heaven and earth. He is in control in this life and beyond.

Then it dawns on me, that's why he chose to take my spouse, to be with him in heaven. He is the Lord of my spouse in heaven. He is also the Lord of me while I'm here in the flesh. What reassurance that is to me at this adjustment time of my life.

There is a spiritual connection between my spouse and me. This connection is endorsed by the Lord God of heaven and earth.

Prayer focus for today: Those who use credit cards indiscriminately.

JUNE 9

My eyes are fixed on you, O Sovereign Lord; in you I take refuge. (Psalm 141:8)

When I look around at my life today, I can be in deep sorrow. My husband and I had so many plans, and now they've gone. I see the familiar household things—his easy chair, his desk, his Bible —and I weep for what is no more. I weep for what can no longer be.

As long as I look around at my life or look back on what was, I will continue to be in sorrow. The Lord reminds me in this verse to fix my eyes on him. When I do this and acknowledge him as my Sovereign Lord, he will provide the refuge I need.

So, just for today, I promise myself that I will stop looking horizontally at what *is.* Instead I will look vertically up to the Lord. I will not take my eyes off him, my sovereign Lord.

Prayer focus for today: Those who have no goals to work toward.

JUNE 10

Show me your ways, O LORD, teach me your paths;
guide me in your truth and teach me. (Psalm 25:4–5)

The death of your spouse may have placed you in the middle of a profusion of crossroads and forks in the road. Which way should you go? Should you relocate? What is the best use for the insurance money? What should you do about filing for Social Security? There are so many possible routes to take.

To make matters worse, recovering from the shock of being left alone can bring with it a blurring of our judgment. We just can't make up our minds on simple things like whether to open or close the draperies. How could we possibly make sound decisions about the big things we face?

We can't make sound judgments on our own. But really, we don't even have to do them by ourselves. The Lord is ready to show us the path. He will guide us. He will point out the direction he has chosen for our lives.

When we can't rely on our own decisions, rejoice. We can depend totally on his perfect direction for our lives.

Prayer focus for today: Police officers and others who enforce the law.

See, I have engraved you on the palms of my hands.
(Isaiah 49:16)

Look at the palm of your hand. What do you see?
Lines? Crevices? A slight indentation in the center of the palm?

Now, imagine that palm is the hand of the Lord.
He told us he has engraved us on it. Can you see yourself snuggled safely there? Try to do that right now.
Concentrate on what a blissful world that would be.

But, as you snuggle deeper into his palm, you feel a
scar on his hand. The child in you may wonder what
happened to it. The adult in you knows exactly what
happened.

The Lord of the universe loves you so much that
he was willing to go far beyond giving you security
and peace in this lifetime. He was eager and willing
to give you eternal peace and salvation by the sacrifice of his Son Jesus Christ. That scar on his hand is
our reminder of that perfect sacrifice.

As you're adjusting to your life alone, snuggle
into his palm, but be vitally aware and eternally grateful for his sacrifice for you.

Prayer focus for today: Those who write music for Christian artists.

JUNE 12

Do everything in love. (1 Corinthians 16:14)

We're called to be loving people. Our Lord and Savior Jesus Christ has mandated that. Whatever we do should have love as its basis.

When I lost my spouse, I found that my emotions were keener than ever. It seems like that is a contradiction in terms, but the Lord allows you to love even when in the midst of terrible grief.

My friends and fellow Christians rallied around me. They brought flowers. They lavished food on me. My church produced the most elaborate luncheon you could hope for immediately after my husband's funeral.

During that time, I was given a rose by each church family. The bouquet almost covered the entire table. Such love!

My gratitude for these deeds done in love was intense. Thanks be to the Lord for teaching his followers to do everything in love.

Prayer focus for today: Older students returning to school.

Do not be wise in your own eyes. (Proverbs 3:7)

This time of year, we think of graduations from high schools and institutions of higher learning. There are diplomas, graduation ceremonies, flowing academic robes, and tasseled mortar boards. Speakers congratulate the graduates and extol the virtues of attaining knowledge.

It's tempting to feel self-sufficient once you have studied hard and successfully attained a degree, or another, and another. The world looks at your framed certificates from universities and says, "Wow! You must really know a lot!"

The truth is that the more you know, the more you realize how little you really know. This is probably the Lord reminding you that you should not be wise in your own eyes.

The only true wisdom comes from God. Trusting in academics and degrees alone does not make a person wise. The person who trusts in God is truly wise.

Today, forget the learning of the world. Don't put your trust in worldly wisdom. Put all your trust in him!

Prayer focus for today: Christian counselors.

JUNE 14

If anything is excellent or praiseworthy—think about such things. (Philippians 4:8)

How good are you with focusing cameras? Those funny little circles that surround camera lenses are, as I dimly understand, a means of focusing the picture so it will be clearer. It's a way of altering how the camera looks at things.

Our lives can parallel that. The way we look at or focus on life determines our perception of things. For example, if we concentrate on happy thoughts, our perception is usually pretty good. On the other hand, if we focus on "what else can go wrong," our attitude can be pretty miserable. As we're told, we should think excellent or praiseworthy things.

That's not easy to do. Right now while we're in the middle of our adjustment to widowhood, it may seem difficult to focus on what is good around us. What's the solution?

Maybe we should pretend we're cameras and let the Master Photographer alter the focus settings so that we can concentrate on the excellent things in life. Instead of saying in our own strength we can't do it, we should yield to him.

Prayer focus for today: A cure for diabetes, and for those afflicted.

You will go out in joy and be led forth in peace.
(Isaiah 55:12)

Those words are promises of good things ahead for those who believe in the Lord. We will "go out in joy." We shall be "led forth in peace." These words in the Scriptures denote the departure from Babylon. Have you heard of Babylon?

There's a lot written about Babylon in the word of God. It was a city devoted to material possession and the pursuit and worship of sensual pleasures. It was not a preferred home for the children of the King. No wonder the Israelites rejoiced when they were finally able to leave there.

Is there a Babylon in your life? Does the world beckon you to come and enjoy secular pleasures? Especially now, in your loss, you may be vulnerable to the temptations of the Babylon you live in. Rebuke those feelings and look for him to lead you forth in peace and into the pure joy of being where he wants you to be in his will.

Prayer focus for today: Blessings on pastors who continue to study the word and remain true to it.

JUNE 16

"It is for God's glory so that God's Son may be glorified through it." (John 11:4)

Do you know when the Lord Jesus Christ spoke these words? If you look at the whole story, you will see that he said them to Martha and Mary when their brother, Lazarus, died. He told them that the reason this happened was so that God would be glorified. You know the ending: Lazarus was raised from the dead and God *was* glorified.

"OK," you say, "fine." But how can you even suggest that God is glorified by the death of your spouse? Your spouse is dead. There was no raising of the dead. Where is the glory?

The glory, my dear child of God, is that your spouse is now in the full glory, the Shekinah glory of the Lord. Your spouse has been raised to a place where there is no more death, only the pure joy of being with the Lord.

For now, cling to that thought, rejoice for your spouse, and wait for God's glory to cover you.

Prayer focus for today: Those who have suffered the ravages of flood.

"The Spirit of the Lord will come upon you in power, and you will prophesy with them; and you will be changed into a different person." (1 Samuel 10:6)

Have you ever seen those little sponges that are only a fraction of an inch thick? When you buy them, they look like a thick piece of paper. Often they are in the shape of a butterfly, a cat, or a house. When you immerse them in water, immediately they become thicker and larger. They become different. They are not what they were, and you can't make them go back as they had been.

Think about your life today as one of those little sponges and think about one symbolic meaning of the water that transforms the sponge. The outpouring of the Holy Spirit is the latter rain as described by Joel. Imagine this latter rain pouring down on those sponges. Instead of letting you remain what you have been, this water from heaven, this latter rain representing the Spirit of God, has changed you.

Maybe this change was not one you planned. One day you were married, the next day you're widowed. But the Holy Spirit still rains on you and is waiting to come upon you in power. Trust that he knows what is best and soak up his latter rain.

Prayer focus for today: Those who support missionaries.

JUNE 18

And my God will meet all your needs according to his glorious riches in Christ Jesus. (Philippians 4:19)

Many of us have trouble with budgeting. Just when you think you might get a little ahead, some unforeseen expense comes up. It can be a challenge!

Now especially, as you're resetting your priorities in the aftermath of your bereavement, you may find budgeting is difficult, if not impossible. How will you ever be able to pay your bills? Will there be enough? How can you afford such and such? Before you know it, you're worrying about finances.

What does the Scriptures tell us? Your God will supply *all* your needs. That doesn't mean all except the rent or the groceries; it means *all* your needs.

He can do this because of his glorious riches. Your Abba Father owns the cattle on a thousand hills. Claim that and watch him do wonders with your budget.

Prayer focus for today: Public defenders in our court system.

JUNE 19

"Whatever you ask for in prayer, believe that you have received it, and it will be yours." (Mark 11:24)

Semantics is the term applied to the meaning of words. Have you ever considered the semantics of a child? The child asks for a toy. The answer is "no." To the child, that "no" means "maybe." The child asks for another toy. This time the answer is "maybe." To the child, "maybe" means "yes." Children assume that the answer to their requests will be what they want.

We may chuckle at this, but think about it. First, we have been told to come to the Lord as a child. Then we're told in this verse that whatever we ask for in prayer, we will receive. It will be ours! He's telling us that his answer to our prayers will always be what we would desire. We need to approach him boldly as a child when we ask. Believe and it will be ours.

What does this say to us today in our mourning time? It says the same thing, dear child of God. Do you need peace in the midst of your sorrow? Pray and believe. Whatever your needs are today or tomorrow, pray and believe. They will be yours.

Prayer focus for today: Parents of students in inner city schools.

JUNE 20

A righteous man may have many troubles, but the LORD delivers him from them all. (Psalm 34:19)

We try to be righteous. We try to do what's right. Then how come we have many troubles? Now in the hour of our mourning, those troubles seem to increase tenfold. Why is this, Lord? Don't you care about your righteous? Don't you care that we now must do everything alone, that the children now have only one parent or that we have troubles all around?

Then he gently points us to the last words of today's verse. The Lord delivers us from all our many troubles. You see, he does care. It's not his choice that these problems are in our lives. But it is his choice to help us safely through them.

So, we continue to trust him. We continue to try to live a righteous life. And we continue to watch how he will deliver us from them all.

Prayer focus for today: Missionaries in third world countries.

Who shall separate us from the love of Christ?
(Romans 8:35)

One word picture of how Jesus comes into your heart suggests that within each one of us there is a vacant spot. This space is the right shape and size for Jesus to inhabit. It is a perfect fit for him. We are cautioned in the Scriptures to fill that space with Jesus. For if we don't, the wiles of the world may take over that vacant area. It is then that we are in danger of being separated from God.

But when we let him into our lives, he actually becomes part of us. Our task, then, is to invite him in so he can live within us.

If he lives in us, who or what can separate us from him? Nothing! Since he lives in us, his life becomes part of our very being.

Even when your life has been turned upside down, you are loved by Christ. Even if you question him and ask, "Why did you take my spouse?" he still loves you. Remember, nothing can separate you from his love. He's part of you.

Prayer focus for today: Those who are homebound.

JUNE 22

I say to God my Rock, "Why have you forgotten me?
Why must I go about mourning?" (Psalm 42:9)

When we're in the middle of our bereavement, this verse could be our theme song. It's easy to ask God if he has forgotten us. We may question why we mourn.

His answer can be as simple as John 11:35, the shortest verse in the Bible: "Jesus wept." How do we dare assume that he doesn't know how we feel. He, too, knew sorrow and mourning.

He mourned when his friend Lazarus died. Since Jesus was the Perfect One, he undoubtedly felt things even more keenly than you or I do. His mourning for his friend was probably more intense than anything we have to go through.

Think of what a miracle it was that he took on our human form and shares in our emotions. He, the God of the universe, who is our Rock, knows how we feel. He would never forget us. All we are called to do is to cling to that Rock.

Prayer focus for today: Those who worry.

JUNE 23

The Lord is faithful, and he will strengthen and protect
you from the evil one. (2 Thessalonians 3:3)

When you feel like you can't go on alone, look to the words in the Bible. There are so many assurances. Maybe he needs to keep assuring us because we're such slow learners. We tend to keep forgetting that he is faithful.

These words from 2 Thessalonians are one of these reminders to us in the hour of our mourning. He gently reminds us of his faithfulness and his strength. All we have to do is reach out to him.

And he promises another thing for us in these words. He will protect us from the evil one. When you feel you're bogged down with woes, it could be an attack from Satan. Reach up to the Lord. With his perfect strength, he will make you strong. He will wrap his hedge of protection around you.

Prayer focus for today: Physicians who volunteer on foreign missions.

JUNE 24

Teach me your way, O LORD, and I will walk in your truth; give me an undivided heart, that I may fear your name. (Psalm 86:11)

Did you have a favorite teacher? Think about how that teacher dealt with you as you struggled to learn. When you didn't quite grasp a point, it was re-explained for you. If you failed to follow directions, you may have been disciplined firmly but lovingly. The final result was that you did learn from the teacher's instructions.

Our Lord works in much the same ways as he lovingly sets out lessons to teach us his truths. He has all the characteristics of a perfect teacher. Right now, in the middle of your tough times, he's using this grieving process as an object lesson for you or someone else.

So ask him to teach you what he will so you can walk in his ways. He's the true favorite teacher.

Prayer focus for today: Pastors in retirement.

JUNE 25

I lie awake; I have become like a bird alone on a roof.
(Psalm 102:7)

The nights are long; the darkness just goes on and on. As I lie there, the bed is so empty. The silence is deafening.

But then I hear a bird on my roof. How did he get there at this hour of the night? No matter, he just did. I hear the rustle of his wings and the swishing of his little feet. The roof has a steep pitch. What if he rolled down the roof and onto the ground? Then it strikes me: since the death of my spouse, I'm like a helpless little bird caught on a precarious place. I may scurry around and try to swish my wings, but the potential danger is there. What if I fall down? Who's there to keep me from hurting myself?

And the answer comes quickly and with certainty: if the Lord cares so much for the birds of the air, how dare I think that he won't care for me?

So when the nights seem long, I picture the little bird in my mind. I thank the Lord for his providential care and go on.

Prayer focus for today: Those who minister to homeless people.

JUNE 26

Trust in him, so that you may overflow with hope by the power of the Holy Spirit. (Romans 15:13)

Have you ever watched preschoolers play with water? They splash and giggle. They fill caps, buckets, and cans. They pour water from one cup to a smaller cup and giggle as it overflows. Such exquisitely complete joy.

As adults, we don't play with water and giggle. Well, maybe we should begin to think as a child of the Lord and about his literal flood of blessings.

Try to imagine yourself as a preschool child at water play. Close your eyes and see yourself pouring water until it overflows. Be a trusting child. That, dear child of God, is exactly how the hope of God will fill you to overflowing. He does this for you by the mighty power of the Holy Spirit.

Prayer focus for today: Pray for those who have never heard about Jesus.

JUNE 27

Be my rock of refuge, to which I can always go.
(Psalm 71:3)

When we're digging a garden, we may not always rejoice when we find a rock in the soil. The rock is immovable. It is solid. It is lasting.

The Lord uses word pictures to explain himself to us. One of those is the rock. He tells us that he, the Lord, is a rock for us. The attributes of a rock are welcome when we think of the Lord: immovable, solid, and lasting.

We may even think of the Lord as a large mass of rock, forming a huge cliff in front of us. This cliff could have insets and caverns in it where we can take refuge when we run to that Rock.

Especially now, as we mourn for our loss, we need to run to the one sure solid thing—the Rock, the cliff, the refuge. He is the only One we can depend on.

Thank you, Lord, for being here for me.

Prayer focus for today: School systems that are receptive to student Bible studies.

JUNE 28

> *Not to us, O LORD, not to us but to your name be the glory, because of your love and faithfulness.* (Psalm 115:1)

You go to the produce department at the grocery store. You see asparagus. It looks good, but the price is a little high. You say to yourself, "I'll grow it myself."

You go to the garden store. They sell you asparagus roots. They don't look like asparagus; they are dry roots. But the label says they are asparagus. You follow the directions, plant them, and then watch. You have to wait a year or two for the roots to produce those glorious shoots known as asparagus. While waiting, you may wonder if anything is happening.

Our Lord's faithfulness to us may at times seem like those asparagus roots. We can't see the potential. We may wonder, "Lord, where are you?" We may question today if we ever will see green shoots of hope. Our assurance of his love and faithfulness is found in Psalm 115. When we are still and patient, his glory is revealed in its fullness.

Remember asparagus roots.

Prayer focus for today: That we may be faithful stewards of what God has given us.

JUNE 29

Trust in him at all times, O people; pour out your hearts to him, for God is our refuge. (Psalm 62:8)

Some people don't want to bother God about the little problems in life. They save their prayers for the biggies. I've even heard spiritual leaders suggest we should save God's grace for the catastrophes.

But what does our Lord tell us? He wants us to trust him at all times. This does not mean only when disaster is ready to pound on you. This means at all times. He cares if your little toe hurts. He cares if you need a parking space. He cares when your heart is broken. He cares that you are bereaved.

So, dear child of God, pour out your heart to him. Let him know how you feel. Tell him you're scared. Share with him that you miss your spouse passionately. Ask him to help you find those car keys.

Thank him for being there for you in all things.

Prayer focus for today: Hospital chaplains.

JUNE 30

I was overcome by trouble and sorrow. Then I called on the name of the LORD. (Psalm 116:3–4)

Have you ever seen those paint-with-water books for children? At first, the picture books look like mere black and white drawings. They're nice pictures, but a little drab.

But when you put a paint brush into water and brush it over those black and white drawings, colors appear. The mere application of water to what once was flat and vacant makes an array of interesting Technicolor pictures.

When our lives are overcome by trouble and sorrow, we are a little like those black and white drawings. Maybe now in this time of your mourning, you feel flat and vacant.

Try to think of using those paint brushes to work as you call on the name of the Lord. He has the power to change what you feel into a myriad of colors.

Prayer focus for today: Children who are motherless.

JULY 1

*That they might be called trees of righteousness,
the planting of the* LORD. *(Isaiah 61:3 KJV)*

When I think of trees of righteousness, I picture tall, sturdy, mighty oak trees. I see these trees growing upward, lifting their branches toward the Lord their creator. They do not shoot up rapidly as weeds or thorn bushes, but grow slowly and steadily.

The roots of these trees of righteousness are large and extensive. Tree roots are roughly the same shape and dimensions of the tree tops. Imagine what an impervious root system that is! These trees are rooted firmly in the Lord Jesus Christ. Storms are not a real threat to trees that have solid roots.

That same Lord Jesus Christ wants us to be trees of righteousness. He gently helps us grow toward him. He is so pleased as we extend our arms or branches upward seeking him. If our growth in him seems slow to us, at least it is consistent and steady. He's patient with us, so should we be with ourselves and with others.

When we are rooted firmly in him, no storm of life, bereavement, guilt, or loneliness can uproot us from our solid Root, Jesus Christ.

Prayer focus for today: Those in adult day care.

JULY 2

*"Do not grieve, for the joy of the L*ORD *is your strength."*
(Nehemiah 8:10)

Grieving and weeping are part of the aftermath in the losing of a spouse. How do you feel after a day of grieving? Exhausted? Tired? Then how do you feel after days or weeks of it? Maybe you feel there are just no more tears left because you don't have the energy to even cry. Don't you wish there were vitamins or a tonic you could take that would help restore your strength?

Good news, dear child of God. There is a tonic that can do that. It's not found on the pharmacist's shelf; it's found within you. You just have to decide to look for it.

When you are born again of the Holy Spirit, Jesus lives within you. Being born again also means you possess eternal life with Jesus. *There* is your joy!

It's understandable if your joy is submerged somewhere under that lake of tears during your time of sorrow. But after the tears diminish, you will once again feel his joy bubbling up in you, slowly at first, but in time it will overflow within you.

Prayer focus for today: Those facing retirement with reluctance.

JULY 3

"For I have not come to call the righteous, but sinners."
(Matthew 9:13)

When a child does wrong things willfully, what is a likely response from the parent? Probably the child is told, "You're bad." When a child is told this often enough she begins to believe she truly is a bad person. "What's the use?" she figures, "Since I'm bad anyway, I might just as well go into the kitchen and steal cookies!"

A more positive way of handling bad behavior is to look at how God deals with us sinners. Our God hates sins. Evil deeds are an abomination to him. Who does these evil, sinful deeds? People! Although God hates the wrong they do, he still loves people. He hates the sin; he loves the sinner.

If we follow the Lord's way, we would tell the child, "You did a bad thing. I still love you, but that was not a good thing to do."

Praise God that he does indeed love us and that our sins are covered by the blood of Jesus. Even if we question why he took our spouses, he still loves us.

Praise him!

Prayer focus for today: Conviction of conscience for the producers of X-rated films.

186

JULY 4

> *"The LORD does not look at the things man looks at. Man looks at the outward appearance, but the LORD looks at the heart."* (1 Samuel 16:7)

My friends look at me with pity. They see the tears. They notice the TV dinners-for-one in my grocery cart. They see me carry purchases into the car myself and drive off alone. They see the empty place beside me at church. They think, "Poor lady, she's a widow."

People only see outward appearances. All they understand is what they can see for themselves. The things they notice are the surface things. They are the things that won't make a bit of difference a hundred years from now.

The Lord sees in me what is important. The Lord knows I am his precious child who just happens to be alone for this brief moment. He knows what makes a difference in the light of eternity. He sees what I'm trying to be on the inside. Through all the grief, I'm confident that in the scheme of forever, this is just a twinkling of an eye.

Prayer focus for today: That our nation truly believes "In God We Trust."

"He has done everything well," they said. "He even makes the deaf hear and the mute speak." (Mark 7:37)

The people of Jesus' time witnessed him performing great miracles. They saw him make "the deaf hear and the mute speak." No doubt, some of them had been praying for those deaf or mute people. Their answer was healing. So they applauded him by saying that he did everything well.

But what happens when our prayers for healing don't work? What happens when our spouse dies despite the fervent prayers and vigils to ask God not to let that happen?

Does this mean that God has not done everything well? Do we withhold applause because he has not done what we asked? Has he really not done well?

Dear sweet child of God, his will is perfect. He knows the end of the story. He knows far better than we possibly could what the best solution is to any situation.

Even if his answer to our pleas is "no," we can still rejoice and know that he does indeed do everything well.

Prayer focus for today: Our judicial system.

JULY 6

Weeping may remain for a night, but rejoicing comes in the morning. (Psalm 30:5)

Did you ever watch a crying two-year-old? The tears and the sobs are real. The distress is genuine. The little one appears to be broken-hearted. Two-year-olds are experts in demonstrating tantrums!

But sooner or later, the child realizes that crying is not fun. It's much more fun to find a ball to play with or join in a game with others. Joy is restored in the child.

So it is with your weeping. There's nothing wrong with weeping. Weep when you must during the night of your grief.

But then turn your weeping over to the Lord. Trust in him as a little child and rejoicing will come in the morning. In his time, the morning will come.

And when your weeping times re-occur, know they are only for a night. Morning is coming.

Prayer focus for today: That Christians truly be the salt of the earth.

"Seek and you will find." (Luke 11:9)

Suppose you need a quart of lowfat milk. Do you sit and wish for it to come to you? Do you find a picture of milk and be satisfied with that? Or do you get into your car, drive to the supermarket, look for the dairy department, and buy that quart of low-fat milk? In other words, do you seek what you need?

It's like that when you need the peace of God. You may long for his solace and for serenity in the midst of the turmoil in your life now that you are widowed. Should you just wish for it or be satisfied with substitute peace or with frenzied activities to fill in your days and nights?

No, my dear child of God, when you truly seek God, you'll see he's been there all the time, waiting for you to realize how very much you need him. Seek him with all your heart, soul, and being.

Prayer focus for today: Those serving our country in the military.

JULY 8

"But as for you, be strong and do not give up, for your work will be rewarded." (2 Chronicles 15:7)

Have you ever watched a road crew paving a highway? It seems roads are usually paved on the hottest day of the year. The crew has to deal with steamy tar plus oppressive heat. But they continue to lay the tar, smooth it, and roll it. When it's all done, they're undoubtedly tired, but their efforts have produced a smooth road for us to travel on.

Our lives can be a little bit like that. We have a task to do. The outward circumstances can't always make that task easy. There can be all sorts of heat we have to go through as we plod along doing what our Lord has called us to do.

This heat could be misunderstanding from onlookers. It could be the heat of being asked to do something we feel we have to stretch to be able to accomplish. The heat could also be fear, anger, or sorrow that saps our energy and tempts us to give up.

But our Lord has promised a reward for us when we persevere. What greater reward could we ask for than being welcomed in eternity with "Well done!"

Prayer focus for today: People having no health insurance.

JULY 9

From the fullness of his grace we have all received one blessing after another. (John 1:16)

One of the marvels of modern technology is the automatic ice maker. The bin is full. You reach in and take handfuls and fill glass after glass of iced tea. When the supply of cubes lowers, you close the freezer door. You hear the sound of the water going through the little tube. Then, you hear the clunk of ice falling into the bin. The next time you need ice, the bin is full of cubes again. What a marvel!

A greater marvel than that ice cube maker is how the Lord's full grace sends blessings upon blessings. Just when we think we have used them all up, there are piles and piles more.

When you lost your spouse, maybe you felt that you had reached the bottom of his blessings and that there are no more. Surprise! He blesses you once again.

Prayer focus for today: Pastors.

JULY 10

He will not grow tired or weary, and his understanding no one can fathom. (Isaiah 40:28)

Do you ever wonder how God can hear each one of us as we pray when you know at any one time there are thousands of others also praying to him? As a human, I can't comprehend this at all. As a believer, I rejoice that my God can do this.

I also rejoice, but can't fathom, why he doesn't grow tired of my endless and repeated requests. I know in theory that whatever I ask for in his name will be given to me. Why then do I keep pestering God?

Is it because of his infinite understanding of who I am because he is my Creator? He takes personal interest because he is my Abba Father. Praise him! He knows what I'm going to ask for even again and again. He cries along with me when I tell him how lonely I feel now that I'm alone. And he never tires of hearing from me.

Praise you, Father.

Prayer focus for today: Clerks who work nights at convenience stores.

Rejoice with those who rejoice; mourn with those who mourn. (Romans 12:15)

F or you math buffs, here's an equation:

$$1 + 1 = 0$$

How can that be, you may say? Here's the explanation.

The "1" equals one person with a problem. Some modern psychologists tell us that when you are down, a solution is to find someone else with a problem. Reach out to help that person and you'll find your own situation doesn't swallow you up.

So the equation written out tells us:

1 person with a problem
+ <u>1 person with a problem</u>
= no problems

Wow, modern psychology, eh? Well, look at today's verse, written centuries ago. Rejoice with others. Mourn with others. Reach out beyond yourself. It's the best antidote for the poison of self-pity.

Prayer focus for today: Those who accept too much responsibility.

JULY 12

Unless the LORD builds the house, its builders labor in vain. (Psalm 127:1)

When your spouse dies, your life as you once knew it is gone. What you felt was stable and dependable is no longer there. It's a little bit like having a house one day and the next day a hurricane comes to dash it to pieces. How do you begin to reconstruct what was?

We're told in this psalm that we should look to the Lord when building our house. The same is true in building our lives. For if we look to our own resources, all our efforts will be useless.

Then how are we to look to the Lord for help in reshaping our lives? He is eager to do this, so we need to talk with him about our plans. When we fervently ask the Lord about relocating or changing careers, he gives us answers by presenting us with situations that answer our questions.

Our job in the rebuilding process of our lives is to spend more time in prayer and more time listening for his answers.

Prayer focus for today: Workers in Mother's Day Out programs.

JULY 13

Consider it pure joy, my brothers, whenever you face trials of many kinds, because you know that the testing of your faith develops perseverance. (James 1:2–3)

Imagine what it would be like to be a kernel of popcorn. You'd be one of many in a row, all part of one ear of corn. You may know you were made to become white fluffy popcorn. But what do you have to go through to become a fully popped kernel? You have to be heated. Whether that heat is air, oil, or a campfire, you have to go through it to become what you were meant to be.

Do you sense an analogy with your life? You are a special child of God. He chose you from all the others to a particular calling. You may have a sense of what you were made for and you see where he wants you to be, but he sometimes needs to put you through a heating process to get you there. Your bereavement is part of that process. Be patient and as joyful as you can be, knowing that it develops you into what he wants you to be, what you were created to be.

Prayer focus for today: Nurses who care for premature babies.

JULY 14

"Do not let your hearts be troubled." (John 14:1)

These days people are concerned about the health of their hearts. Videos and programs abound so you can exercise your cardio-vascular system. Even fast food restaurants give you information on the nutritional elements in their offerings so you can make healthy choices.

There's nothing inherently wrong with caring for your heart. But the true cardiac specialist is the Lord. He is the one who knows the cure for whatever ails you.

For example, is your heart troubled? Is it broken since you lost your spouse? Turn to the one who can heal you, Jehovah-Rapha, the healer. He alone can take your troubled heart and restore it to the strong, healthy status he wishes for you.

Prayer focus for today: Malicious gossipers.

JULY 15

He will satisfy your needs in a sun-scorched land and will strengthen your frame. (Isaiah 58:11)

You're traveling down a road on a hot day. You see on the road ahead what looks like a shiny pool of water. As you get closer, you see that it was only a mirage.

A similar phenomenon can happen to those who are in a desert. You've no doubt read of the experience. But in the desert, there are real pools of water that offer respite to sun-parched travelers. These pools are known as oasis. An oasis is not a mirage, or false haven, but rather an authentic haven.

When we're in the desert of our lives, we really need to know there is an oasis out there for us. Especially at this bereavement time, we need reassurance from our Lord that he is there.

He would never subject us to the false hope of a mirage. Never would he taunt his children like that. What he offers is the real thing—cooling, refreshing solace.

So dear child of God, don't feel you're in a dry arid place for the rest of your life. Keep watching and see the peace and comfort he is so eager to give you.

Prayer focus for today: Those who are desperate for love.

JULY 16

Carry each other's burdens, and in this way you will fulfill the law of Christ. (Galatians 6:2)

My older son is a lacrosse player. He really enjoys it and works hard to fine-tune his skills in the sport. His mother, however, is a klutz. All I know about lacrosse has been absorbed vicariously. If I understand correctly, there are players who end up with assists. Sometimes a player is applauded for saves. In short, it's a team sport. To win, it is vital that each player works to help the others.

The Bible also tells us to be team players. We're instructed to carry each other's burdens. Isn't this like playing lacrosse? We can help each other reach the goal of salvation in Jesus. All of us need encouragement from others who are with us in the game of life. At other times, the encourager may be the one who needs assistance.

While we're still in our time of mourning, we may need to have more of our burdens carried by others. It's OK. We're not weaker lacrosse players because of this. We just need someone to assist us. Praise God for providing those for us.

My prayer is that soon we will be strong enough to assist others.

Prayer focus for today: Those who make decisions about conduct in business.

JULY 17

"Arise, shine, for your light has come, and the glory of the LORD rises upon you." (Isaiah 60:1)

Are you a morning person or an evening person? Was your spouse an evening person while you were a morning person or vice versa? It's interesting to think how often marriage partners are exact opposites in their peak times of day.

Now that your spouse has died, do you find that your "morning/evening" personhood has changed? I found that to be the case. My husband always rose early, did his morning devotions, then woke me for our morning prayers together. Now that he's gone, I find myself rising earlier. Maybe it's to recapture those moments when he would have been up. Maybe it's because I now have the responsibility of doing everything myself—the bill paying, sweeping the porch, taking out the trash, etc.

But I have found in rising earlier that the mornings are glorious. Our Lord provides magnificent sunrises. He sets the birds to singing for his children when they awake. The Lord himself wants to greet his children with the light of his presence.

Prayer focus for today: Those in mental institutions.

JULY 18

> *May God himself, the God of peace, sanctify you through and through.* (1 Thessalonians 5:23)

Water is a concern in our modern world. You see bottled water in all the stores. Companies who tout the virtues of their filtering systems flourish. Hardware stores sell devices that supposedly filter out impurities. Grocery stores have dispensing machines where you can fill up your own containers with spring water.

This concern is well-founded. We need to take measures to protect ourselves against contaminants. But there is a far more important purity that merits our attention: the sanctification of being holy.

Being sanctified means to be set apart for sacred use. To honor our holy God, we should seek to be as pure as we can be so we can be used by him. We should filter out any contaminants that taint that sanctification. Being sorry for ourselves, being angry at God for taking our spouse, or being fearful about the future are all impurities we should seek to filter out of our lives.

When we seek to do this, God promises to restore his peace in us, his sanctified children.

Prayer focus for today: Thanks for freedom of worship.

JULY 19

"I am the L<small>ORD</small>, who exercises kindness, justice and righteousness on earth, for in these I delight," declares the L<small>ORD</small>. (Jeremiah 9:24)

L ord, it's hard for me to understand why I'm left alone. I thought that you wanted what's best for me. Surely being widowed was not your first choice. Or is this just a cruel set of circumstances? You do care, Lord, don't you?

And then you remind me of these words from Jeremiah. You say you delight in kindness, justice, and righteousness. You say you exercise these virtues. Where do these virtues fit in with what obliterated my life as I knew it?

Then you have to remind me further. You say, "I am the Lord." As Lord, of course, you're very aware of how devastated I feel right now. Since I am your child, you grieve along with me.

And as Lord, you do exercise kindness, justice, and righteousness to me in your perfect timing. Lord, one more thing I ask of you: patience for me to see all you do for me.

Prayer focus for today: Teenagers seeking jobs.

JULY 20

Sing and make music in your heart to the Lord, always giving thanks to God the Father for everything, in the name of our Lord Jesus Christ. (Ephesians 5:19–20)

Playing the accordion is a rare skill. But this extraordinary instrument can be an object lesson for us.

Think about it. How does the accordion produce music? If it just sits there, no sound can come out of it. It is only when the accordion is put in its proper place and *squeezed* that it does what it was manufactured to do. Out of the "squeeze box" comes music.

Our lives are a lot like the accordion. If we just sit here, we accomplish nothing. Frequently he has to squeeze us to make the music he placed within us. We may not like it. We didn't ask to be widowed. We may be uncomfortable and wish there had been another way. But he still does whatever squeezing is necessary for us to make music in our hearts to him.

Prayer focus for today: Understanding and peace in the Middle East.

*"See, the former things have taken place, and new things
I declare; before they spring into being I announce them
to you."* (Isaiah 42:9)

The former things have taken place! Nobody
knows that better than those of us who are widowed. We are painfully aware that things aren't as they
once were. We're reminded of this when we see letters
still addressed to "Mr. and Mrs." We notice that the
laundry now only consists of our belongings. There
are still people who don't know and ask innocently how
your spouse is doing. The former things are gone!

But our Lord never does something blindly. He
has a greater purpose for what he chose to do. He has
promised that there are new things ahead for his dear
children. We may see this situation as *what he has taken
away.* Our Lord may see it as *what he plans to do for us.*

Our role in this is to acknowledge that our lives
are changed, but also to look ahead to new things we
never dreamed of before.

Prayer focus for today: Vacation Bible School leaders.

JULY 22

> *"If you do not stand firm in your faith, you will not stand at all."* (Isaiah 7:9)

Remember those little black and white rectangles called dominoes? They have lots of potential for games. The main idea is that you match the numbers of white dots to others, making a pattern somewhat similar to a black and white crossword puzzle.

However, years ago some ingenious person discovered you could stand these black rectangles on end. They can be put close together to create wavy paths. When these masterpieces of paths are complete, you push over the first and all the rest fall down in a continuing pattern. There are even some self-proclaimed experts who spend days devising intricate ways to set up the dominoes.

Think of these dominoes. They stand erect and firm until someone tips over the first one. Our lives are like that. We're told if we don't stand firm, we are in deep trouble. Standing firm means we don't let life's little setbacks make us waver.

We need to stand firm in spite of our circumstances. Don't be a domino!

Prayer focus for today: Traveling evangelists.

We live by faith, not by sight. (2 Corinthians 5:7)

People may say, "How do you know your God is real? Have you ever seen him?" The reply we cling to is, "We live by faith, not by sight."

The widow of Zarephath from 1 Kings 7 can be our role model. If you recall the story, the widow had only a handful of flour and a little oil. It was all she had between her and total starvation.

The prophet Elijah, sent by the Lord, asked the widow to bake him some bread using her last ingredients. He told her that the Lord God promised that her flour would not be used up and her oil would not run dry.

She probably looked at what she had but chose to live by faith, not by sight. She baked the bread for Elijah and even had enough to bake a small loaf for herself and her son.

From that day on, her supplies never ran out. She had lived by faith, not by sight. Can we do the same?

Prayer focus for today: Our President and his staff.

JULY 24

> *Do not hide your face from me when I am in distress.*
> (Psalm 102:2)

In my days of bereavement, I may go around murmuring that God is hiding his face from me. I may be so sorry for myself that I'm just positive God is looking the other way.

But then I look around me, where I am, in my house. Then I realize that I have been so engulfed in my own grief that I just don't recognize his face. God really is with me. He shows his face in the sun peeking through the window, in the compassion of others, and in those shivers of joy that come upon me unexpectedly.

Then I go outside into the brilliant sunlight and walk down the street. I see! When I look into myself and grieve that God is hiding from me, it's like looking at a tall building on a sunny day. You don't see the sun. It's there. It's just that it's behind that building. When I forget that earthly building and look up, I see the sun, the symbol of my perfect Lord.

Thank you Lord for showing me you've been there all the time!

Prayer focus for today: Blessings on those who care for aging parents.

JULY 25

Therefore, as we have opportunity, let us do good to all people, especially to those who belong to the family of believers. (Galatians 6:10)

The Lord asks us to do good to all people, but we are called particularly to take care of those who are in the family of believers.

One way of looking at this family of believers is to think of it as actually being the body of Christ. You've no doubt heard teachings of Christ having no hands but yours. We are called to be the hands and the feet of Christ as we go through our journey here on this earth.

So what does that mean? Think of all believers as being one body in Christ. Other parts of your body send assistance to help ease the pain of a stubbed toe.

It should be that way within the church. If one has a hurt, the others know it and rally around the hurt member.

I pray that you experience the body of Christ coming to care for you when you are bereaved. I also pray that you will do that for someone else.

Prayer focus for today: Hurricane victims.

JULY 26

He has caused his wonders to be remembered; the LORD
is gracious and compassionate. (Psalm 111:4)

The mighty deeds of our Lord are countless. They are incomprehensible to the mind of most humans. Our God knows that, so he uses everyday experience to remind us of his mighty deeds.

For example, he gives us gravity. Without it, we would fly off into space somewhere. He gives us air to breathe, so we can continue to live. He gives us the sun to warm us and cool breezes to refresh us. He provides food and water for us.

In daily experience, he reminds us of his wonders and power. As we go through our days and weeks of adjusting to our widowed status, he reminds us that he is in control by allowing us to see him work through everyday things.

Prayer focus for today: Owners of small businesses.

JULY 27

My flesh and my heart may fail, but God is the strength of my heart. (Psalm 73:26)

What happens to a glass of soda when it sits for an extended period of time? The bubbles that show its carbonation slowly begin to dissipate. Soon your glass of soda is flat. It has lost its fizz.

Do you feel your life right now is a little like that glass of soda? It once was fresh and bubbly, but now you're alone and you feel flat with no fizz.

You could go around from now on staring at the flat glass of soda. Or you could look to what the psalmist tells us. He says our flesh and heart may fail, as did the carbonation in the soda, but God is the strength of our heart.

So it really doesn't matter if your soda has gone flat. That's only the flesh part. You can go on and reach out to God who is the true source of strength.

His power never loses its fizz.

Prayer focus for today: Service personnel who are stationed overseas.

JULY 28

Man is like a breath; his days are like a fleeting shadow.
(Psalm 144:4)

What is a breath? It's fragile and short-lasting, and then it's gone. The psalmist tells us that man is like that. No one knows that better than those of us who are widowed. We are painfully aware of how quickly a life passes on to eternity.

But praise God, that's not all there is. The story doesn't end with the short-lived breath or fleeting shadow. We have an eternity for us to live in where there are no fleeting shadows and where we will live forever in the pure Light of the Lamb.

So, we grieve as we must for the fleeting life of our spouse. But we rejoice that the endless days of no separation, no death, and no grief are coming!

Praise God!

Prayer focus for today: Those who have power and control over large sums of money.

His name is the LORD—and rejoice before him. A father to the fatherless, a defender of widows, is God in his holy dwelling. (Psalm 68:4–5)

When you start to think that no one cares about you or the fact that you've lost your spouse, look to what the Scriptures promise us. We are assured that the Lord is our Abba Father. He is there to take you up into his lap and be your protector, like your daddy. What a blessed thought! The God of the universe cares so deeply for just you. He is the perfect, absolute father to us all.

The Word further assures us that he is a defender of widows. Those who are bereaved have a special place in the heart of our Lord. He weeps with us. He'd surely prefer that we didn't have to go through this time, but we live in an imperfect world, and death is part of that imperfection.

Our God lives in his holy dwelling, a place of utter perfection. When we are called to shed our imperfect earthly bodies, we will enter his holy dwelling to be with him forever.

All memories of the unhappiness of this world will be obliterated.

Prayer focus for today: Patients in cardiac care units.

JULY 30

*I consider everything a loss compared to the surpass-
ing greatness of knowing Christ Jesus my Lord.*
(Philippians 3:8)

Those who are true connoisseurs of coffee would
say that only brewed coffee is acceptable. Those
of us who are content with the instant variety don't
recognize the difference. But to a coffee expert, drink-
ing instant coffee would be disgusting. It's really a matter of the "real thing" as opposed to an "imitation."

St. Paul alluded to the real thing versus anything
less when he wrote this verse as part of his letter to
the Philippians. He said he considers a loss anything
less than knowing Jesus Christ as Lord. This was
Paul, formerly Saul of Tarsus, talking. Paul, who was
well educated and held renowned status as an envied
citizen of Rome, considered all his credentials as
nothing. All he gloried in was his Lord Jesus Christ.

Dear child of God, try to put yourself in a similar frame of mind. Anything you may have or have
had in the past, including your marriage, pales in the
light of who Jesus is.

Prayer focus for today: Moms and Dads who seek to
refine their parenting skills.

So Abraham called that place The LORD Will Provide. And to this day it is said, "On the mountain of the LORD it will be provided." (Genesis 22:14)

You know the story. The Lord gave Abraham a son, Isaac, a child of the promise. But then one day, the Lord asked Abraham to go up to the mountain and sacrifice Isaac. Abraham must have been resentful, but he obeyed anyway. He took Isaac up to the mountain and prepared to kill him. The Lord stopped Abraham and provided a substitute, a ram, to be the sacrifice.

Abraham called the place "The LORD Will Provide." People still say, "The Lord will provide," and that's true; he will take care of us. But look where Abraham had to go and what he had to be willing to do. He had to determine he would do as he was instructed to do. He had to go up on the mountain to carry it out.

Are you willing to go where the Lord tells you to go? Would you be so ready to sacrifice whatever he asks?

Prayer focus for today: Publishers of church school curriculum materials.

AUGUST 1

And let us consider how we may spur one another on toward love and good deeds. (Hebrews 10:24)

At this time of your life, it is very easy to curl up in a corner and feel sorry for yourself. It's not that sorrow itself is bad. Feeling sorrow is an emotion which our Creator built into us, so it must be blessed by him.

But our Creator also gave us spiritual gifts. Think of the gift of encouragement. Ah! There you have a way to pull yourself out of the corner and beyond the tunnel vision of "poor me."

An encourager who truly uses the gift given by the Lord seeks ways to inspire or stimulate others to be what the Lord planned for them to be. You could say an encourager is a sort of spiritual cheerleader.

So, when you're tempted to sit in your little tunnel and dwell on your loss, dust off the megaphone and cheer others on.

Prayer focus for today: Autistic children.

Shout for joy, O heavens; rejoice, O earth; burst into song, O mountains! For the LORD comforts his people. (Isaiah 49:13)

Try to picture yourself out in a glorious expanse of an unspoiled area that is still in the condition it was when the Lord created it. Overhead you see the blue, crystal-clear skies with billowing wisps of clouds. The earth is covered with lush green grass and decorated with wild flowers of variegated colors. All around, gigantic purple mountains strain to reach into that blue sky.

After you've used your mind's eye to imagine this, try using your mind's ear to theorize what magnificent music this creation could make. The heavens shout for joy, the earth rejoices, and the mountains burst into song.

And the reason for all of this is to show that the Lord comforts his people. So when your soul is craving comfort, picture and hear in your mind the glories of the Lord's creation. With this he provides balm for your hurting soul.

Prayer focus for today: Blessings on those who study the Word faithfully.

AUGUST 3

This is the day the LORD has made; let us rejoice and be glad in it. (Psalm 118:24)

Today is the anniversary date of the day my husband died. In my mind, I keep replaying the events of that day—the high fever, calling 911, the emergency room, seeing him so ill he didn't recognize me, being ushered into a "quiet room," hearing the doctors say, "He's gone." It's a bad time of year for me.

At least, I keep thinking it's a bad time, but the Lord reminds me that he made all "times" and all he made is good. He tells us this is the day he made. Rejoice and be glad in it.

And I do rejoice. When I stop thinking about how bad a time it is for me, I remember how good it is that he gave me this day. He is eager to put rejoicing in my heart, so he will make me glad.

Thank you, Lord, for making this time of year for me.

Prayer focus for today: Pray for the moral fiber of television programming.

AUGUST 4

"The Lord knows those who are his." (2 Timothy 2:19)

A lot of people wear crosses today. You see them in shops at the malls—simple crosses on tiny gold chains, embellished crosses on heavy chains. Why do people wear them? Generally speaking, wearing a cross symbolizes to the world that you're a Christian. Therefore, when someone puts one on, it is a witness to the Lord's sacrifice for us. It can also be a reminder of him to the person wearing it. In a sense, wearing a cross marks us as Christians.

When the Lord comes to call his elect, will he look only for those wearing crosses? I rather doubt it, don't you? He knows those who are his. He doesn't need any of our earthly trappings to tell him who really is born again. He knows because he knows because he knows!

Perhaps the Lord doesn't need earthly adornments to be able to figure out who is his. But we, as mere mortals, need to be reminded. We are the ones who need them.

If wearing a cross gives you assurance, that's fine. Just remember, he knows your heart and can see beyond items and circumstances.

Prayer focus for today: Inner city mission churches.

AUGUST 5

Oh my Strength, I watch for you; you, O God, are my fortress, my loving God. (Psalm 59:9)

L ord, *I* feel so weak. *I* can't eat. *I* can't sleep. *I* can't do anything. *I* have so little strength left. *I* wonder how *I* can go on. *I* am grieving, Lord.

Then you point out something very significant. Look at the number of times *I* appears in what I just said. Each sentence began with *I*. And all the sentences were negative, talking about what *I* can't do.

You're right, Lord. When I depend on myself, I can't. But when I look to your Word and repeat these words from the psalmist, I realize where my strength comes from.

Lord, *you* are my strength. *You* are my fortress. *You* are my loving God.

When I think of you this way, I am assured that you never intended for me to go through this grieving process on my own strength.

Praise *you!*

Prayer focus for today: Thanks for all the saints who have gone before us to pave the way.

AUGUST 6

"Therefore do not worry about tomorrow, for tomorrow will worry about itself. Each day has enough trouble of its own." (Matthew 6:34)

That great philosopher Scarlett O'Hara said, "I'll worry about that tomorrow."

We think, what a wise statement. But, you know, someone upstaged Scarlett by saying the same thing. Jesus himself told us two thousand years ago not to worry about anything.

If we allow ourselves the latitude to wait until tomorrow to worry, we'll never worry because tomorrow is never today. It is tomorrow.

How wise our Savior was to teach us not to be concerned about anything beyond today. It's a little bit like being faced with eating a roasted elephant. How could you accomplish such a task? One spoonful at a time.

Deal with the task for now. And leave the worrying for tomorrow.

Prayer focus for today: Those who are serving our country on the seas.

220

AUGUST 7

> *But I pray to you, O L*ORD*, in the time of your favor;*
> *. . .Rescue me from the mire.* (Psalm 69:13–14)

People, look at me and marvel at how well I'm
doing. Sure, I have it all together. I've taken care
of the immediate details and arrangements. I am re-
arranging my living. For some people I might be
termed "cool."

But deep down, I feel like I'm sinking in mire. This
is an old descriptive word for deep mud or slush.
Many times, as I try to be strong in my bereaved state,
the mire of sadness and loneliness threatens to pull
me down and under. It gets tougher and tougher to
keep lifting my feet to pull out of it.

The Lord reminds me when I pray to him that he
has the solution. He has the perfect heavenly davit to
keep me out of the mire. In the time of his favor,
which means he is very near, he is ready to reach out
and rescue me.

Thank you, Lord.

Prayer focus for today: Unforgiving people.

AUGUST 8

"Whoever follows me will never walk in darkness, but will have the light of life." (John 8:12)

You said if I follow you, I will *never* walk in darkness. Then why have I fallen into this black hole, this pit of melancholy? Why did you take my spouse and leave me in this pitch dark?

And then you remind me of this verse, "Whoever follows me will never walk in darkness, but will have the light of life."

That's what I'm forgetting, Lord. You promised that your light is always there. So I'm really never in the darkness as long as I focus on your light.

Forgive me, Lord.

Prayer focus for today: Those with infertility problems.

AUGUST 9

> *Yet he gave a command to the skies above and opened the doors of the heavens; he rained down manna for the people to eat, he gave them the grain of heaven.* (Psalm 78:23–24)

Are you afraid of the future? Do you wonder how in the world you're going to survive? Do you suppose the children of Israel felt that way, too? We're told in the Scriptures that they were a worrying bunch.

Did the Lord forsake them in all their worrying? Of course not. He was their Abba Father. He provided for them in a miraculous way. He sent manna. Scholars of today try to explain away manna, but the bottom line is that it *was* a miracle from God, specifically for his people at the time they needed it.

If the Lord provided so dramatically for the children of Israel, will he do any less for you, dear child of God? He knows your worries. He is ready to care for all you material needs.

Watch for his manna.

Prayer focus for today: Conviction of conscious for false prophets.

Jesus replied, "You do not realize now what I am doing, but later you will understand." (John 13:7)

These words were spoken by Jesus as he prepared to wash the feet of Peter, one of his disciples. What was Peter's response? "No, Lord, you mustn't do that!" You see, Peter, in his typical foot-in-the-mouth manner, thought he knew what was best.

What was the Lord's response? "Even though you don't see why now, you will understand *later.*" Do you feel you don't understand why the Lord has put you in this position now? Do you, like Peter, protest, "But Lord? Why? You shouldn't have let my spouse die."

Dear precious child of God, we in our human, our less-than-perfect forms may not realize what he's doing. But he promised that *later* we will understand.

When is later? It may be in this lifetime, or in the eternal understanding of the next lifetime. Our role is to sit back, be patient in what the Lord needs to do, and be ready to comprehend what he has done for us, whenever that later is.

Prayer focus for today: Young children who need to have their boundaries set.

AUGUST 11

*"He will call upon me, and I will answer him; I will
be with him in trouble."* (Psalm 91:15)

These words recorded by the psalmist were spoken
by the Lord God. He tells us to call on him,
assures us he will answer, and promises to be with us
in trouble.

"Sounds good," you may say, "but how about
when I came home to an empty, dark house? Is he
really with me then?" The answer to that depends on
whether you believe, truly believe, his words or not.

Dear child of God, you may *feel* you're alone, but
you *know* you're not. He's with you when you call to
him. In fact, he's with you even before you call to
him. He's there all the time.

Maybe he just wants us to acknowledge this by
suggesting that we be the ones to call on him. When
we do, we are admitting we're afraid, or lonely, or helpless. He may not need to be asked to help us, but he
knows *we* need to ask.

So, boldly approach his throne with your calls for
help in your loneliness.

Prayer focus for today: Those with responsibility to
guard the incarcerated.

And as for you, brothers, never tire of doing what is right. (2 Thessalonians 3:13)

Doing what is right can encompass activities that are good for us. We try to eat the right foods. We engage in exercise programs. We get proper rest and fresh air and avoid harmful habits. It can get tiresome, can't it?

Shortly after my husband died, I saw a bumper sticker that proclaimed, "Eat wisely. Exercise. And die anyway." Some say that's sick humor. I say, "Ain't it the truth!" You see, my husband was careful about his diet. He was involved in strenuous exercise outside in the fresh air. He was in great physical shape. And yet, he contracted an anaerobic bacterial infection and died anyway.

What's the solution here, dear child of God? Are we to give up and be fatalistic in taking care of ourselves? No, he expects us to do the best we can.

But we are not called to rely on physical health; we are called to rely on him. We are called to tirelessly do the best we can and to seek what is right.

He'll care for us no matter what the outcome.

Prayer focus for today: Those who are facing moral temptation.

AUGUST 13

The LORD lifts up those who are bowed down, the LORD loves the righteous. (Psalm 146:8)

Worshipping the Lord is a real joy. When we truly lose ourselves in adoring the Mighty God of Israel, we can almost see him walking the aisles of the church or circling around as we give him praise.

"That's fine," you may say, but today as you still grieve, you don't feel very worshipful. You may feel bogged down by the millstone of your bereavement. Do you suppose the Lord understands?

Dear child of God, he confirms that he lifts up those who are bowed down. This means he is right there with us, circling around us, wanting to take us in his powerful arms to comfort and elate us. Yes, he does understand when you feel you can worship or when you feel you cannot.

He loves you, the righteous.

Prayer focus for today: Single mothers of preschool children.

AUGUST 14

Finally, be strong in the Lord and in his mighty power.
(Ephesians 6:10)

Do you frequent health food stores? A lot of people do today. It's amazing how the proper numbers and amounts of vitamins and minerals can increase your energy and sense of well-being.

These stores sometimes carry elixirs of some form or another which purport to give you even greater strength. Now, this is admirable. But, there is only one inexhaustible source of strength and power. That source is the Lord alone.

So, when you feel exhausted by all the adjustments singleness requires, use the earthly elixirs when necessary. They're fine for helping you deal with the stress.

But remember to praise the source of all strength and power.

Prayer focus for today: Biblical scholars.

AUGUST 15

You are my lamp, O Lord; the Lord turns my darkness into light. (2 Samuel 22:29)

This verse uses the analogy of a lamp to describe the Lord. Let's think of it as an oil lamp. In our mind's eye, let's look at that lamp while it's still daylight.

First, we see a glass bowl container. Inside we see the reservoir of oil. The oil has a sweet fragrance so we can smell it with our mind's nose. The reservoir of oil is ready when it's needed.

There's a fabric wick that reaches down into that ready source of oil. And there's a knob which has the capability of turning the wick higher or lower so the size of the flame can be adjusted.

The lamp is ready before it gets dark. And when do you really need and appreciate the lamp? When the darkness sets in. That's when the lamp turns the darkness into light. All you need to do is avail yourself of its light.

Sound a little like your life today? When the darkness of sorrow surrounds you, the Lord, our lamp, is ready, prepared, and waiting to give you light.

Prayer focus for today: Those who long for companionship.

AUGUST 16

As a father has compassion on his children, so the LORD *has compassion on those who fear him.* (Psalm 103:13)

There once were three little girls. They loved to play Monster with their daddy. They would beg him to play the game over and over again. The daddy would hide and then chase after them. The little girls would squeal and run off in a state of excited fear.

But the daddy had a role in this that was far more in depth than just being the monster. He had to watch out for possible dangers that could harm the little girls—slippery throw rugs, corners of the fireplace hearth, and glass doors.

He probably remembered from his own childhood how easy it was to get hurt. So, he was being a daddy with compassion for his little ones.

Our heavenly father cares for us much the same way. He knows from the experience of his Son what we're going through. So, he takes special precautions to keep us safe. He knows or has compassion for us in our sorrow because he was there when his Son died for our sins.

Praise him for his unfathomable compassion.

Prayer focus for today: Homeless people.

AUGUST 17

"The LORD has afflicted me; the Almighty has brought misfortune upon me." (Ruth 1:21)

These words were bitterly spoken by Naomi. She not only was a widow, but she also had lost her only two sons to death. She was in Moab, a land far away from home, and probably felt the Lord's affliction very deeply. She lamented that she had no more possibilities for other sons. Mournfully, she set out to return to her homeland. One of her foreign daughters-in-law chose to stay in Moab. The other, Ruth, chose to go with Naomi to her homeland at Bethlehem.

Naomi continued to grieve. She and Ruth, the two widows, settled in Bethlehem sadly.

However, the Lord knew the ending of this little story and had a greater plan in mind for Ruth and Naomi. He provided for their sustenance through a kinsman, Boaz. In time, Boaz and Ruth were married. From that union came Obed, a son that Naomi could vicariously claim as hers. And the culmination of this story is that Obed was in the direct lineage of the savior Jesus Christ.

If you are feeling the Lord has brought misfortune upon you, think of Naomi. She felt much as you do. Look what the Lord did for her. Can you expect any less?

Prayer focus for today: Farmers.

*For God did not give us a spirit of timidity, but a spirit
of power, of love and of self-discipline.* (2 Timothy 1:7)

How good are you at pretending? Just for now, give it a try. You're a teeny-tiny tugboat, and you have the job of towing a gigantic cruise ship. You look down at your small but sturdy frame and then you look up at that white, glistening vessel. It's enough to make you extremely tired.

You're pretending to be that tugboat, but think about it. Do you sometimes feel small and unsure, looking up at that gigantic task ahead? Maybe that task involves legal aspects of your spouse's death. Maybe it's financial uncertainty. Maybe those tasks make you timid.

But look, dear child of God, he gave us a spirit of power, love, and self-discipline, not a spirit of timidity. This is his assurance that we can do whatever tasks loom in our lives. So, be a tugboat and pull with all your might. You have the power of the Almighty God on your side!

Prayer focus for today: Those who give generously to the work of the Lord.

AUGUST 19

> *"The LORD is my strength and my song; he has become my salvation."* (Exodus 15:2)

Lord, you tell me that you're my strength. Well, today I don't feel very strong. I feel like a weak human caught in the mire of mourning. You also tell me that you're my song. I don't feel much like singing. I am sorrowful.

Maybe I'm like a guitar that's out of tune. There's something very sorrowful and depressing to hear a guitar with strings that are not in proper tension. The notes just don't sound right.

When a guitar is out of tune, what's the solution? "Tuning it, of course," you say. How do you tune it? One way is to tune the guitar to itself. You strike one string and then, by using a system of touching the frets, you can tune each string to the previous one.

But a far more scientific and reliable way is to use an electronic tuner. This device gives you an accurate reading by measuring the sound. You can see on the gauge precisely when the string is tuned correctly.

Can you see an analogy between the guitar and your life today? We tend to go around in our sorrow, measuring ourselves against ourselves. It would be preferable to tune ourselves to a Perfect One. That one is Jesus. Keep yourself in tune with him. You'll be surprised at the strength he gives you and the songs you can produce together.

Prayer focus for today: Those who are in danger from weather emergencies.

"The righteous will live by faith." (Romans 1:17)

There's a story about an atheist who asks a Christian, "What will happen if when you die, you find out all your belief in Jesus just isn't true?" The Christian replies, "It won't be as bad as when you die and find out that my belief in Jesus is true!"

That's what the righteous live by, their faith. No matter what happens. In the good times, in the not-so-good times, the righteous continue to believe. It's the adrenaline that keeps them going.

If your life isn't exactly as you wish it could be, hang on to your belief in Jesus. The story isn't over yet. Don't let the weights of the world pull you down.

Continue to live by faith.

Prayer focus for today: Short-term missionaries.

AUGUST 21

May your good Spirit lead me on level ground.
(Psalm 143:10)

Most experts agree that walking is almost the perfect exercise for everybody. And that's fine when you have access to a safe walking track. It's also fine as long as the weather cooperates; we tend not to walk well in rain, snow, or ice.

One solution is to use a treadmill. You can regulate the speed so you're walking at a pace which is best for you. You're walking, in a sense, on level ground.

It's possible to elevate the incline on some treadmills. This gives you more of a challenge and is probably more realistic. After all, few walking areas are absolutely flat. There are hills and valleys, ups and downs.

Aren't our lives a little like that? We may wish our treadmill would keep us only on level ground. But reality dictates that we will find ourselves facing hills and valleys. We surely have felt those ups and downs while dealing with bereavement.

But our Lord is sufficient. He promises his Spirit will lead us to level ground.

Prayer focus for today: College students away from home for the first time.

AUGUST 22

Be joyful in hope, patient in affliction, faithful in prayer.
(Romans 12:12)

Did you ever notice how many sermons have three points? That may be all our finite minds can comprehend. Assuming this to be true, look at the three points Paul is suggesting in today's verse.

The first is to be *joyful.* Well, that's easy to say, but right now you may not be bubbling over with glee. You're down and joy is just not an abundant part of your life.

OK, then go to point number two, *patience.* You may wonder how the Lord expects you to be patient when there are so many details that scream, "tend to me now." There seems to be no end to your hours of waiting for comfort. Patience is just not one of your virtues right now.

Then we look at point number three, *faithful.* The Lord wants us to be steadfast, especially in prayer to him. It is in our faithfulness to him that we will find patience and joy. So, do you see how these points interrelate?

Our lives are like that. If one part seems out of synch, strive for what you can do. Soon you will find completion.

Prayer focus for today: Those using the gift of hospitality.

AUGUST 23

Trust in the LORD with all your heart. (Proverbs 3:5)

We say we trust the Lord, but what does that mean? Some synonyms for trust are confidence, belief, and hope. Do we have complete confidence in him? Do we believe in him without reservation? Is our hope in him and him alone?

We answer, "Yes, Lord." He then asks us to show him by giving ourselves to him completely. He wants our life to become a living sacrifice to him. His choice for us is that we trust him so completely that we're willing to be a living sacrifice. However, the problem with living sacrifices is that they keep crawling off the altar.

Do we see ourselves crawling off that altar? Do we say we trust God in all things except_____? The minute we say "except," we are limiting the power in our lives. We are not trusting him with all our heart.

While you're in your grieving process, you may feel it's more difficult for you to trust completely. Be gentle with yourself. Your loving God understands. He is gentle with you. He is waiting for you to trust him unreservedly.

Prayer focus for today: Rest and peace for travelers.

For what is seen is temporary, but what is unseen is eternal. (2 Corinthians 4:18)

Look at the clouds against a blue sky. Do those clouds always look the same? Of course you know the answer to that. Clouds are constantly changing shape, size, and form.

It can be amazing to watch as a puffy cloud looking like a marshmallow changes into one that looks like a smokestack. Sometimes a lot of little clouds join together to make one big blob. Clouds don't stay the same, nor do they stay in one place. You could say they are temporary. What makes the clouds move, change, or disappear? The answer, dear child, is the unseen wind.

Wind, in the Scriptures, is one description of the Holy Spirit. *Ruach* is the Old Testament word for this wind. The Holy Spirit may be unseen, but the results of what he does can be seen and felt.

When you see the clouds as they move across the sky, be thankful for the Holy Spirit who helps us blot out our temporary discomforts so we can rejoice in what is unseen and eternal.

Prayer focus for today: Clients of crisis pregnancy centers.

AUGUST 25

> *May your love and your truth always protect me.*
> *For troubles without number surround me.*
> (Psalm 40:11–12)

Since the death of my spouse, I've had to face things that I never gave a fleeting thought to before. There are probate and taxes. The car insurance now rates me as "unmarried." There are bills that don't seem to end. And then there's the loneliness and the grief. I didn't vote for this! It's true, troubles without number surround me.

As long as I dwell on my troubles, I feel this. And then I'm reminded of the first part of this verse from Psalm 40. It assures me that the Lord's love and truth always protect me. It doesn't say they will protect me. It is in the present tense. They *always* protect me. This means it's done. It's ongoing.

So I praise you, Lord, for your love and for showing me the truth that you are always there with me no matter how many troubles the world may send my way.

Our God is greater than any number of troubles. Praise him.

Prayer focus for today: Publishers of Christian books.

Nothing in all creation is hidden from God's sight.
(Hebrews 4:13)

The world today seems to be full of people who are getting away with something. There's money laundering. Officials in high offices shred sensitive documents. Cheating on income tax returns seems to be excusable because "everyone does it." Court cases are thrown out because of inadmissible evidence. Charlatans are lurking to take advantage of the bereaved. From the world's eye, they are indeed getting away with it.

Are they really? In the final analysis, at the judgment, are they getting away with it? Of course not! Nothing is hidden from God's sight. He sees and knows all and has it all under control.

In the same way, he sees and knows all about us in our time of sorrow. Even that is under his control. We may feel that we are easy prey for those who take advantage of us and cheat us, but God is in control. He sees. He knows. He's there to protect us.

Thank you, Lord.

Prayer focus for today: Children who have lost a sibling to death.

AUGUST 27

For from him and through him and to him are all things.
(Romans 11:36)

A preschooler leans over to contemplate a marigold in the garden. "What makes that flower stand up?" he wonders. To answer that question, with a typical childlike action he pulls up the entire plant.

There at the base of the plant are the roots. "Funny," he thinks, "I didn't see them before." He takes the uprooted marigold to his mother.

His mother uses that as a teaching to explain that Jesus is our root. Just as the root is necessary for the plant, we too need to have our lives firmly based on Jesus, the true root. For it is *from, through,* and *to* him that all things have their being.

Pretend you are that little preschool boy. Be thankful that Jesus is the root of your life. No matter what storms of life arise, you are firmly held by him.

Prayer focus for today: Christian college students attending secular schools.

"I will build you up again and you will be rebuilt."
(Jeremiah 31:4)

Have you ever lived through a house fire? It's not a pleasant experience. In fact, it's devastating to see flames shooting up through the roof of your house. The smoke permeates everything. The water used to douse the fire runs over everything.

When the fire itself is out, you face the destruction it caused. Walls fall down. The roof caves in. There's dirt, smoke damage, and water everywhere. Just looking at it can make you think your life has fallen apart just as your house has fallen apart.

Maybe you feel your life has fallen apart because of the death of your spouse. You look around you and sorrowfully see the destruction of what once was—your life as you knew it. It will never be the same again.

That's true. It won't be the same as before. But he promised he'd build us up again. Just as the house can be restored after a fire, a little differently than before, so our lives will be re-formed. They will not be the same. They are changed by the Lord. All we're called to do is allow him the freedom to go about his business of doing what he knows is best for us.

Prayer focus for today: Tornado victims.

AUGUST 29

We take captive every thought to make it obedient to Christ. (2 Corinthians 10:5)

I was walking in the mall one day. Idly I found myself wandering into a novelty store. The trinkets were intriguing, even amusing. The jewelry was the usual costume stuff. There were even some battery operated toy dogs that jumped in circles.

I walked farther back and there were shelves full of adult games and novelties. They were overtly sexual. There were reminders of that part of my life that is no more.

I got out of that store as fast as I could. As I continued on my walk, I wondered just why there have to be so many reminders of sex to taunt those of us who have lost a spouse. It's not just the novelty store. It's in advertisements, on the television, everywhere. Sex sells, they say.

It's difficult, Lord, not to let my thoughts center on grieving for my sex life that is no more. Please help me take captive every thought, especially thoughts about sex. Please help me make all of my thoughts and all of my life obedient to you Lord.

Prayer focus for today: Christian youth programs that reach out to the inner city.

I pray that you may be active in sharing your faith.
(Philemon 6)

There is a measure of freedom in being single. You surely were called to do the work of the Lord with your spouse when you were part of two. Now you're free to do some of the tasks the Lord may be calling you to do alone.

If you're afraid, that's to be expected. Your security may have been because you were part of two. Your focus on your security needs to shift upward a little, toward the Mighty God of Israel.

He's calling you to share your faith with others. "Wait just a minute," you say, "I'm afraid, Lord; I'm afraid I'll offend someone."

Offend someone? By telling them about Jesus? Which is worse, to offend someone who chooses not to listen or to offend the One who asks you to tell others about the Greatest One who ever lived?

You see, dear child of God, there's no contest here. He's calling you to be active in sharing your faith. Trust him. Set out in faith and the assurance that you are doing what he alone calls you to do alone.

Prayer focus for today: Congregations seeking pastors.

AUGUST 31

Let us hold unswervingly to the hope we profess, for he who promised is faithful. (Hebrews 10:23)

The canoe smoothly drifted down the river. It was so peaceful. The sky was clear blue overhead. Trees along the shore nodded their heads and waved their leaves in the gentle breeze. It was idyllic. The only sound was the steady swoosh of the paddles as the two riders in the canoe made their way down the river.

But suddenly, there was a different sound. Gurgling, bubbling, splashing water ahead. Rapids were coming up. The two in the canoe steered the craft between two rocks, and suddenly they were caught in the rapids. The canoe turned sideways and smashed into a protruding rock. The canoe tipped and both riders tumbled out into the gurgling, bubbling rapids.

When the canoe stuck on a rock, the canoeists held on and called for help. In a short time, other canoes came down the river. They loosened the canoe and rescued the two who were holding unswervingly to the rock.

Do you see the way the Lord works in this little anecdote? We are told to hold on unswervingly for he is faithful. The canoeists did that and were rescued by a faithful God sending help.

If he did that for these two, do you think he'll do any less for you?

Prayer focus for today: Those who would use violent ways to make a statement.

"That he might be glorified." (Isaiah 61:3 KJV)

Years ago, there was a craze for 3-D movies. To get the full benefit of this presentation, you had to wear special glasses provided by the movie theater. When you looked through them, the action on the screen had an added dimension of depth. People would squeal with delight (or horror) as missiles seemed to come out into the theater itself. They experienced the picture in three dimensions.

Now consider how we may think of God in this light. We may have gone through these dimensions as he led us gently into a deeper understanding of who he really is.

First, we accepted that God is God. That's one dimension and an important basis for what follows. You can think of that dimension as horizontal. When we begin to praise God, we add a vertical dimension. We reach upward with our adoration of him. We are seeing him in two dimensions. But, when we glorify him, truly give him the honor due him, his glory fills the temple of our hearts and we experience his power in greater depth, adding a third dimension.

We should seek this 3-D glorification of him especially now at this time of our grief. When we glorify him in all three dimensions, he enters our lives with healing balm.

Prayer focus for today: Churches who offer Christian schools.

SEPTEMBER 2

Praise our God, O peoples, let the sound of his praise be heard; he has preserved our lives and kept our feet from slipping. (Psalm 66:8–9)

I f you've been to one of those renovated zoos, you may have seen an exhibit of the ibex (mountain goat) in a replica of its native habitat. You probably saw a small mound built inside the exhibit. The sides of this mound were steep, rocky crags. The ibex stands on these rocks and makes its way up or down these slopes with astonishing skill. It can do this because the creator of our universe made the ibex sure-footed to keep it from slipping.

If our Lord can do that for the ibex, imagine how much more he desires that you, dear child of God, should be sure-footed. Even when you look down and are frightened about the future, your financial concerns, and the years of loneliness you face, he keeps you from slipping. Even if you feel sorrow or grief, he still holds you firmly on the solid rock that is Jesus.

So, make yourself sure-footed on the mountainside where he placed you today and praise him. Praise him so loudly that it echoes across the mountains and resounds on those rocky paths. You need never be afraid again.

Prayer focus for today: Those suffering from Chronic Fatigue Syndrome.

The Spirit helps us in our weakness. (Romans 8:26)

Going to the gym today? If you're with it, you'll be part of an exercise program. Seems like everybody's doing it these days.

So, we work hard with aerobic classes, stair steppers, and exercise bikes. We estimate calories burned while we feel the sweat rolling down our backs. We feel great!

There's nothing inherently wrong with these behaviors. If we truly understand that our body is the temple of the Holy Spirit, then we'll care for it. But relying on externals will not make us strong. Relying on the spirit that dwells within is the only way to attain strength.

And we do need strength right now in the midst of our widowhood. So starting today, let's resolve to let his Spirit build our spiritual bodies.

Prayer focus for today: Blessings on those who produce films for family audiences.

SEPTEMBER 4

You hold me by my right hand. You guide me with your counsel. (Psalm 73:23–24)

Lord, you tell me you'll hold me by my hand. You also tell me you will guide me. Does this mean you want me to step out and try to walk on water? Will you hold my hand and guide me? But, Lord, what if I falter? What if I look around at the raging sea around me? What if . . . ? I feel so vulnerable especially right now as I try to get used to being widowed. Surely, Lord, you don't expect me literally to step out on water right now.

Then gently you remind me that it is possible for me to do that, but later. For now, you ask me to raise my hands in worship toward you. You want me to reach up to you, my Abba Daddy, for you to hold my hands. In private devotions and in public worship, you want me to reach up to you.

And you want to guide me with your counsel. You provide this through your servants who are pastors. Help me, Lord, to listen to what you have to tell me through them.

Praise you, Lord, for holding my hand and for your counsel.

Prayer focus for today: Evangelism efforts in Islamic countries.

SEPTEMBER 5

God is not unjust; he will not forget your work and the love you have shown him as you have helped his people. (Hebrews 6:10)

When we are thrust into the state of being widowed, we may want to be left alone. Our preference would be to shut all the doors and windows, close the drapes, and sit in our chair in the corner . . . alone.

There may be times when we need solitude. But our God made us social creatures, so I doubt that he wants us to spend the rest of our lives alone in our darkened corner.

He tells us in his Word that we are to help his people. We may not feel like doing this right now. After all, we're still in mourning.

But he keeps nudging us to reach out and help others. He has someone call us to ask for a ride to church. He sends our way a child who needs a hug. He brings to us persons who just need to talk over their problems.

And before we know it, our sorrow has lessened. It hasn't evaporated, but it's more bearable because we were obedient to God's call.

Prayer focus for today: Unrepentant people.

SEPTEMBER 6

Give me a sign of your goodness. (Psalm 86:17)

Back in Genesis at the time of Noah, rain was unheard of. As Noah was building the ark, the people of the world scoffed and said, "The weather is going to do what today?" They had no frame of reference for the torrents of water that would come pouring down from the sky. They just didn't understand how it would be.

Before I was widowed, I didn't fully understand how it would be. I may have had the concept, but I surely didn't have a frame of reference.

But then it happened to me, suddenly, without warning: death's finality. It was as if those torrential rains were pounding down on me. Through the salty tears rolling down my cheeks, I could almost feel the deluge. As I sobbed, I thought I would never see the sunshine again. As I sobbed, I thought it would be like this for the rest of my mortal life.

But just as God gave Noah a rainbow as a sign of his covenant, he gives us a spiritual rainbow. Daily he reminds us that he wants us to live in the Sonshine.

Thank you, Lord, for your rainbow.

Prayer focus for today: Those who feel lost in the midst of raging technology.

"Shall we accept good from God, and not trouble?"
(Job 2:10)

L ord I know that your desire for us is good things.
After all, you've created a world with clear blue
skies, soft green grass, and refreshing air to breath.
You want and have given to us what is good.

Job knew this, too, as he said in the verse for
today. He acknowledged your goodness, God. Even
when his earthly possessions were ripped from him,
he clung consistently to praising you, Lord, for your
greatness and sovereignty.

It is hard to recognize your sovereignty. When
you choose to send what we perceive as good, we are
glad. When you choose to send what we perceive as
troubles, we look for what you're trying to teach us.

Troubles have been defined as discipline that
ends in spiritual gain. When we think of troubles as
a tool for our spiritual growth, we can praise the
Lord for it all. When our "trouble" revolves around
our bereavement, we can look for growing closer to
the Lord because of it.

Prayer focus for today: Volunteers who teach in adult literacy programs.

SEPTEMBER 8

So we fix our eyes not on which is seen, but on what is unseen. (2 Corinthians 4:18)

If you look through the large ends of binoculars, you will find something interesting. Instead of simply enlarging things, the items in your vision appear much smaller and distorted. Our eyes could cause us to think that's the way things are.

Maybe your life is a little like that today. You're trying to focus on what's ahead, but all you see is loneliness, fear, boredom, and guilt. Perhaps you're looking through the wrong end of the binoculars.

What's the remedy? Surely you can figure that out for yourself. Try turning the binoculars around and looking ahead. What you once saw in a distorted way will then be comprehensible.

Living in the Spirit is like looking through these binoculars. Try it; focus on the unseen. Don't let the troubles of today rob you of the joy that the Spirit has waiting for you.

Prayer focus for today: Parents of autistic children.

"In days to come you will understand it clearly."
(Jeremiah 23:20)

I don't understand, Lord. Why did you take my spouse? We had so much more living to do together. Why did you do this?

After all, you're the Great Physician. You could have done something. You protect and care for your sheep. Where were you when tragedy threatened? When tragedy struck?

And then your voice comes to me: "You will understand, later. You will see my reasons clearly, later. It may be soon or when we meet in eternity, but I will explain it all. Only trust me."

So thank you, Lord; you are omniscient. You know what is best. So if I don't understand now, be patient with me. I look forward to those days when I will understand clearly.

Prayer focus for today: Those who need friends.

SEPTEMBER 10

He provides food for those who fear him; he remembers his covenant forever. (Psalm 111:5)

O ne of the most wearisome chores of modern living is doing the grocery shopping. At this time of our lives, while we're still adjusting to being widowed, it can be extremely exhausting.

You have to select which brands to buy. Guessing how much is another challenge since there's one less to buy for. You see a favorite food, and the tears begin to flow again. But you have to eat, so you have to do the shopping. The Lord promises he will provide food for us. So we need to rely on his good guidance as we go up and down the aisles of the supermarket.

When the Lord promises us food, he means more than for our bodies. He is ready to provide us with sustenance for our souls and our minds, the food that is lasting. His supermarket is always open and there is no waiting in line. All we have to do is go to him and ask for what he is so eager to give us.

Praise you Lord.

Prayer focus for today: Those who doubt.

"And in this place I will grant peace," declares the LORD Almighty. (Haggai 2:9)

When your spouse died, did you feel like running? I spoke with the widow of a military pilot. She said as she walked behind the casket on the way to the National Cemetery, it was all she could do not to run off screaming through the fields.

At times like this, we may feel we'll never know peace, especially at this place. Our once familiar surroundings painfully remind us of our spouse. We have to walk through the kitchen where we ate breakfast together. It hurts to go to church, alone. Maybe running away is a good idea after all!

And then the Lord reminds us that he will grant peace *in this place.* It is his desire that we stay where we are for now. He'll wrap his arms around us, dry our tears, and let us rest our head peacefully on his shoulder. He may call us to go somewhere else later, but today he wants us to stay and bask in the peace he promises for us right here.

Prayer focus for today: Parents of children in public schools.

SEPTEMBER 12

"For my thoughts are not your thoughts, neither are your ways my ways," declares the LORD. (Isaiah 55:8)

Before your spouse died, how did you think about your marriage? If you're like most of us, you had settled into daily living routines and didn't really think too much about it. Sure, there were misunderstandings to work out. There may have been disagreements about money or children. But these could be addressed and you went on. Your lives together just went on. You didn't have to think about it.

And then it was over. One moment you're married, the next moment you're not. The Lord blesses us at times like that with numbness, a state of not being able to think much beyond the moment-by-moment grief.

Now that the numbness is beginning to wear off, you may begin to question God: "Why did you take my spouse? I thought we'd have more time. I don't understand, Lord."

Then he shows you in his word what he says on this very subject. His thoughts are not our thoughts. His ways are not our ways. The bottom line is that he is in control, and he knows with infinite wisdom what is best for all of us.

Thank you, Lord, for your wise thoughts and ways.

Prayer focus for today: Families whose income is not sufficient to meet their needs.

The LORD is with me like a mighty warrior.
(Jeremiah 20:11)

Remember the fairy tales you read or heard as a young person? There were lovely young maidens who were in danger of one sort or another. And there were dashing young men who conquered any and all adversaries. The lovely young maidens would sigh with delight and swoon over their champion protectors.

"That's nice," you may say, "but that just isn't done these days."

But, dear child of God, those things are done these days. We have the ultimate champion protector: the Lord Jesus Christ. He is the mighty warrior who has fought the ultimate battle on our behalf and has rescued us from the pits of hell. Hallelujah!

Just imagine how easy it is for him to rescue you from the pit of doubt, sorrow, or anger. He can do it. All you have to do is reach out to him and let him defend you.

Prayer focus for today: Children confined to wheelchairs.

SEPTEMBER 14

Set your minds on things above, not on earthly things.
(Colossians 3:2)

My husband was a forester. In our house, we had a bathroom in the laundry adjacent to the doorway from the garage. We used to laughingly refer to this as the "decontamination chamber." He would shower, change his work clothes, and drop them in the laundry before he came into the house.

Shortly after he died, I was cleaning that bathroom. As I scoured the shower stall, I was on my hands and knees and I looked at the silvery drain in the shower. There was a small amount of hair strands, his hair. I scraped them together in a little mass and choked back the tears. It was all I had left of him.

Then the Lord gave me the grace to remember that even those last remaining fragments of him are earthly things. My husband now has a glorified body. So my challenge is to not look around for earthly reminders of him, but to look upward for assurances of the heavenly reminders of him.

Prayer focus for today: Prideful people.

Be still before the LORD and wait patiently for him.
(Psalm 37:7)

Lord, you tell me to be still. How can I? There are
so many details to take care of. I'm the only one
now to remember to pay the electric bill, to water the
yard, to balance the check book, to . . . There's just so
much to do. I can't be still. After all, you want me to
be a responsible adult and there's so much to do.

Then you ask me to wait patiently. How can I wait
and be still when I'm the only one to take care of the
house, the car, the garden? Is it because I'm allowing
my busyness to get in between you and me? Am I hiding behind the electric bill or the vacuuming?

So, just for today, I'll straighten the papers on my
desk and walk away. I'll put the vacuum cleaner away
and I'll close the curtains so I can't see the garden
and the yard.

And I will determine to be "still" and spend time
with you.

Prayer focus for today: Evangelism to the Lord's Chosen,
the Jews.

SEPTEMBER 16

> *"For the sake of his great name the* LORD *will not reject his people, because the* LORD *was pleased to make you his own."* (1 Samuel 12:22)

When your spouse died, you probably were surrounded by people. They brought food. They brought flowers. They screened phone calls for you.

And now, months later, they aren't around anymore. It's understandable. People have their own lives to live. They can't take the time to be there and hold your hand twenty-four hours a day. It could be easy to feel rejected.

But then as you consider the total picture, what is most important, is that they *did* come when your need was urgent. They were following the lead of the Lord who was there too and *has never left you.* He has the time to spend with you. He has made you his own adopted child. He would never reject you, his precious child.

So, rejoice because you are his own. You carry the Name of the Most High God.

Prayer focus for today: Those who are abusers.

"As a shepherd looks after his scattered flock when he is with them, so I will look after my sheep." (Ezekiel 34:12)

There's safety in numbers, they say. Probably sheep feel the same way. Imagine you are a sheep. It must be terrifying to be alone somewhere out on a hillside. Strange noises echo in the night. You wonder where or how many predators are out there ready to take advantage of you in your situation.

But praise God, the Shepherd comes to look after you. He seeks you wherever you are and brings you back to where he can keep an eye on you. He cares for you with tenderness.

Since you lost your spouse, you may feel like a lost sheep. It's easy to be terrified when you're alone. Strange noises make you wonder who or what is there. Charlatans are eager to benefit from your loss.

Who is here to take care of you? Our Lord, the Perfect Shepherd, is looking for you where you are. He wants to bring you safely back into the fold where he can care for you.

Relax, let him who is able take care of you, his little sheep.

Prayer focus for today: Older students working to attain their high school diplomas.

SEPTEMBER 18

> *They were all amazed at the greatness of God.*
> (Luke 9:43)

"God is great. God is good. And we thank him for our food," recites the young child when asked to say grace at meals. But does that child *really* understand that God is *great?* For that matter, do we really understand that greatness of God?

How great is your God? Great enough to have created a universe? Great enough to provide for all your daily needs? Great enough to assure you that all your todays and tomorrows are safe in his hands?

You bet your sweet life he's that great and more! He's great enough to take on all your sorrow, grief, worry, and apprehension and cover you with his complete comfort and solace. He is so great that he cares about all those feelings you have. He's not shocked by any of them. In his infinite greatness he cares.

Our response to this greatness should be one of astonishment, of wonder, and of amazement. How could the great God of the universe care so much for you? Be amazed and give him all the glory.

Prayer focus today: Those who face important decisions.

SEPTEMBER 19

God is our refuge and strength, an ever-present help in trouble. (Psalm 46:1)

Most people enjoy the beach. Crashing waves, salty air, and even the gritty sand please ocean lovers. The sunshine is part of being at the beach, too. Years ago, it was thought to be really good for you—vitamin D and all that. Now the scientists tell us that sunlight is not always kind to our skin.

So what do you do? You want to be at the beach. But the rays of sunlight are a definite danger. You cover yourself up as protection from those rays. First you probably start with sunscreen. You cover your exposed areas with the highest number lotion you can find. Then you cover yourself with sweat suits, towels, a big brimmed hat, and sit under a huge umbrella. In a sense, you are creating a refuge for yourself to keep you from possible trouble caused by too much sunlight.

There is a refuge promised to us in the Scriptures as well. It keeps us safe from any troubles that come our way. That refuge of course is our God, the Mighty One of Israel. So if worries, loneliness, and sorrow threaten you, run to your refuge, your Abba Father who is always there waiting for you.

Prayer focus for today: Believers in Christ who have fallen away.

SEPTEMBER 20

"That joy is mine, and it is now complete." (John 3:29)

L ord, I'm not in the pits of sorrow. Thank you for that. But now I'm numb. How long will I be in this unresponsive state? Will I ever have my emotions back again? Will I ever know happiness?

Then you remind me of your words. You tell me to hang on to them. Repeat after me:

"That joy is mine."

"That joy is mine."

"That joy is mine."

I begin to feel better. Maybe life still holds something for me. You remind me to keep delighting in you. As I keep focusing on that, I find that the gladness I feel in you begins to grow and grow.

Before I know it, my spirit is lifted and it is my true pleasure to praise you!

Prayer focus for today: Rebellious teenagers.

The second son he named Ephraim and said, "It is because God has made me fruitful in the land of my suffering." (Genesis 41:52)

Remember the story of Joseph? He was envied by his brothers, sold into slavery in Egypt, falsely accused, and wrongly jailed. But through it all, Joseph remained faithful to God. And God remained faithful to him.

The end of the story is that Joseph was honored by the Egyptians. He was put in a position of importance. It was his being in this position that made him a vehicle for the deliverance of Israel from starvation. God was faithful not only to Joseph, but to his chosen people.

Even though Joseph considered Egypt the land of his suffering, he realized there were benefits and reasons for this. Joseph named his second son Ephraim, which in Hebrew means fruitful, as a remembrance of God's providential care.

In our time of mourning, do we seek an Ephraim in our lives? If we look, we will focus on the fruits the Lord is eager to produce in our lives.

Prayer focus for today: Instructors in Christian schools.

SEPTEMBER 22

"Where I am, my servant also will be." (John 12:26)

I n the world of business, there are two kinds of employees. One feels they work *for* the company. The other feels they work *with* the company.

What's the difference? Those who work *for* the company tend to see their jobs as a way to make money and get benefits. They spend the required time at work and that's the end of their interest in the company. However, those who work *with* the company want to do all they can to assure the success of the organization. They may study the products made and suggest ways to better them. They may work extra hours or take work home voluntarily, all to be of assistance to the company.

Jesus asks us to be workers for him. Which kind of worker do you suppose he prefers? The one who "puts in time" or the one who is an integral part of his ministry?

Of course the answer is obvious. Now that you are single, you have more time to devote to working for the greatest organization the world has even seen, the Kingdom of our Lord Jesus Christ.

Prayer focus for today: Children with learning disabilities.

"I know your deeds, your hard work and your perseverance." (Revelation 2:2)

They say that as huge as an iceberg is, only ten percent of it is visible above the water. Ninety percent is hidden and can't be easily observed.

What you can do for the Lord can be like that iceberg. The things you do—singing in the choir, working the soup kitchen, or teaching Sunday School—are what the world watches you do. But those things are like the visible parts of the iceberg, about ten percent of what the Lord knows you do.

He knows about your private, daily devotions. He is there when you sit with an ill person. He hears the prayers you utter throughout the day. He listens when you talk to him as you drive down the road alone in your car. No human knows, but he does.

He knows the depth of your mourning, too. Others may assume you're doing fine, but he knows of the lonely nights and your concerns for the future. Trust him with the ninety percent the world doesn't know about. He is sufficient to take care of it all.

Prayer focus for today: Moms in Touch who pray for school children.

SEPTEMBER 24

Seek the LORD while he may be found; call on him while he is near. (Isaiah 55:6)

While we're going through the bewilderment of losing a spouse, contradictory emotions race through us. One moment we feel numb, the next we find our senses to be painfully intense.

For example, I have a favorite song we danced to while dating which brings tears whenever I hear it. I cry when I play audio tapes of our short-term mission trip to South Africa. I hear his clear tenor voice singing in praise with the congregation and I weep.

I see something new, a recently opened road and I think, "I must tell him about . . ." and then I remember! I catch a whiff of shaving lotion, and it reminds me of him. The scent of pine trees brings memories of his hours of work with our Christmas tree farm.

I feel the terry cloth bath towels that he used. They still have the scent of the insect repellent he used while he worked outside. I taste a new food and think, "He'll like this."

The Lord gave me all these senses—hearing, sight, smelling, touch, and taste. They're part of my very being. He understands, yet he asks me to seek his face. What I need to do is turn all my senses toward him, listen for him, look for him, and reach out to touch him.

Prayer focus for today: Those who feel they are in dead-end jobs.

May the LORD *make you increase, both you and your children.* (Psalm 115:14)

Think of a cultured pearl. How is it made? A grain of sand or other irritant gets in the soft inside of an oyster. To protect itself, the oyster forms layers upon concentric layers of nacre around the irritating intrusion. The result of these layers is a lustrous creation we know as a pearl, something very valuable.

We all have intruding irritants in our lives. You may feel your current status of singleness is an irritant. Think of what you can do to turn this problem into something else. Our Lord tells us he wants to increase us. Is this possible?

The best way to work to cover the irritating status of your grief is to cling to our Lord Jesus Christ. As we do this, he will cover the grain of sand with layers and layers of his grace. The result will be an increase in our relationship with him. This is infinitely more valuable than pearls.

Prayer focus for today: Christians who are persecuted for their beliefs.

SEPTEMBER 26

For the Lord will be your confidence. (Proverbs 3:26)

If you live in an area where electrical power outages occur, you know the inconvenience of doing without lights. You are unable to cook. You worry about the frozen food if the outage goes on for an extended period of time. It can be annoying. It can even be unnerving when it becomes dark.

You try to make the best of it until the power is restored. You use flashlights and candles. You try not to think about how dark it is outside of the range of your artificial light.

And then the power is restored. What relief! You appreciate every little light switch, the refrigerator hum, and the radio even more because of the darkness you had been in.

To believers, the Lord can be compared to the restoration of electric power. Once you were in the dark. Now you see the True Light. He is your confidence. And now if you feel in a twilight because of your sorrow, keep looking for the restoration of his power. You have his assurance it will happen.

Prayer focus for today: Christian bookstores.

The promise comes by faith, so that it may be by grace.
(Romans 4:16)

People say to me, "How can you be so sure of what you believe?" or "Have you always been this religious?" or "I don't see how you're so calm since you lost your husband."

First of all, I did *not* lose my husband. I know exactly where he is and whom he is with. I know that with every fiber of my being. I am calm because I have that assurance. I am sure of what I believe because the Lord's promises come by faith.

"Faith is being sure of what we hope for and certain of what we don't see" (Hebrews 11:1). The Lord does not give empty promises to his children. And I know whose child I am!

I do not consider all this as being religious. I consider it truth from my Abba Father who knows me better than I know myself.

He also knows that my faith can be tested by circumstances and feelings. He understands if I falter in my resolve to believe and to know. He's ready to fight the darts of doubt thrown by the enemy.

That's his grace by which we are saved. And his grace strengthens my faith.

Prayer focus for today: Students in private schools.

SEPTEMBER 28

> *A time to weep and a time to laugh, a time to mourn and a time to dance.* (Ecclesiastes 3:4)

These days it seems as if everyone has a daily calendar or planner. We have to check our schedules, pencil in appointments, and call to confirm meeting times. In a sense, we are trying to regulate time.

But time is totally in the hands of the Lord. He alone decrees the number of our days, and he alone decrees the times for weeping, laughing, mourning, and dancing.

If this is a day for you to weep or mourn, know it's from the Lord and that his timing is perfect.

If the Lord gives you a day filled with laughter and dancing, be glad. Take it as a special blessing from him to you, his precious child.

Whatever this day holds for you, remember you are living in the Lord's perfect schedule for you.

Prayer focus for today: Those who give pediatric care.

I sought the LORD, and he answered me; he delivered me from all my fears. (Psalm 34:4)

Lord, where were you when my husband became suddenly ill? Where were you as the anaerobic bacteria rapidly invaded his body? Where were you when fever raged throughout him? Why do you allow mindless organisms to attack your people? Why is there no cure for what he had? Why did you let him become ill so rapidly that we didn't have a chance to say good-bye?

I'm full of questions for the Lord. Where? Why? How come? I pound my fists like a two-year-old and sob, "It's not fair!"

Then the Lord gently reminds me that he's been there all the time. He is in perfect control of my life. He was in perfect control of my husband's life. Each of us has an appointed time to die. All my questioning and fist pounding are just evidence of my lack of understanding.

My responsibility then is to settle down and acknowledge the prevenient grace of my Savior. He's been there all the time.

Prayer focus for today: Blessings on those who seek to fill the fatherless void in the lives of children.

SEPTEMBER 30

> *For we are God's workmanship, created in Christ Jesus*
> *to do good works, which God prepared in advance for us*
> *to do.* (Ephesians 2:10)

On the surface, life may appear to be meaningless. We may even wonder why we were born. But when you're a child of God, born-again into his kingdom, you know you are here for a very specific reason. That reason is to glorify God and enjoy him forever.

When you think of your being as having been planned by God, it changes your outlook. You are, as the Scriptures tell us, God's workmanship. What a powerful thought! He delights in what you are and what he's creating you to be.

We are created in Christ Jesus, his perfect Son. There's power in that also! We are created to do good works. And he's there to show us how to do his good works.

We are not here by chance. Nothing that happens to us is by chance. Our joys, our sorrows, and our situation today are all part of his divine plan.

Prayer focus for today: Chronic headache sufferers.

You anoint my head with oil. (Psalm 23:5)

Just imagine the Lord anointing you with oil. It would feel delightfully warm and soothing as it flows over your head and down your body. It's the balm of Gilead. It is the Lord's blessing upon you.

Anointing with oil in the Scriptures was a sign of being set apart and marked as a special blessing to the world. So it is with you now. Even in your time of trouble, you are set apart. You are being shaped into a special blessing.

Oil was also used by the elders in the New Testament when they were called to pray for the sick. The oil was a healing balm. Christ's anointing can heal you today.

So, wait expectantly for the pure joy of his anointing. It will set you apart. It will soothe your aching heart. Praise be to God for his anointing!

Prayer focus for today: Mothers Against Drunk Driving (MADD).

OCTOBER 2

"For where two or three come together in my name, there am I with them." (Matthew 18:20)

Where are you, Lord? I feel so alone. You said you'd always be with me, but I don't feel you at all today.

If you don't *feel* the Lord is with you right now, don't rely merely on your *feelings.* Instead, try following his concrete directions to come together in a group of two or three.

What does he mean by that? Small groups, dear friend, praying together and joining with others in his Name. And what does he promise in this verse? *There am I.* He is with you there in your prayer group with others who share your faith.

Now especially you need to be with fellow believers to share and to pray. The Lord knows you and your needs. He will communicate with you as you share openly with two or three other believers. If you've been part of a small group, stay with it. If not, resolve right now to seek a group of others who can be your support for this time and for later.

Prayer focus for today: Parents who need guidance in raising their children.

OCTOBER 3

The LORD watches over the way of the righteous.
(Psalm 1:6)

The Lord promises that he watches over us. He keeps a close eye on the paths we choose to take. When necessary, he provides signs to help us choose the way he would want for us.

The signs we see on the roads of today can be reminders of the directions the Lord has for us. A stop sign keeps us from possible danger. A "rough road ahead" sign warns us to drive a little more cautiously. A school crossing sign tells us to be more alert so we can watch out for others who can't watch out for themselves.

One of the signs we often see ignored is the yield sign, yet it's a perfect reminder to us of how we should live our lives in relation to the Lord watching our comings and goings.

Yielding to the Lord means no questions asked, just yield to him. There's no room for our demanding, "Why can't we go faster or in a direction we choose?" We have been called to submit to him. We may not understand or see the reason. We just obey.

Today, keep that picture of the triangular sign in your mind. Concentrate on yielding!

Prayer focus for today: Those who volunteer in times of emergency.

OCTOBER 4

Live as children of light. (Ephesians 5:8)

Lord, those storm clouds are gathering again. They make the sky gray and blot out the sunshine. Today despair is upon me. I don't feel your warm sunshine.

On cloudy days, it is easy to assume the sun is hidden. But frequently, what happens?

The rays of the sun cannot be contained. They shine down through gaps in the clouds and deliver beaming rays of golden light upon the earth below.

Our Lord is like that sunlight. He is perfect Light. Even when we, in our finite minds, are sure that he is hidden from us by the clouds of this life, he breaks holes through the clouds and beams down upon us.

In this, your time of feeling covered by clouds, try to think of those rays of sunshine from your Father. *You* are his child. He loves you dearly. He grieves with you and is communicating with you in those rays of light.

Prayer focus for today: Those diagnosed as terminally ill.

Commit to the LORD whatever you do, and your plans will succeed. (Proverbs 16:3)

We were told when we were growing up that we needed to act our age. We were expected to face things and not act like babies. Now that we are parents or adults in charge, we are presumed to approach perfection.

As adults, people assume that our decisions are right. Others expect that our actions are those of a truly together person. It gets a little wearisome, doesn't it? Is there a solution, especially now when we don't exactly feel like a truly together person?

The answer can be found in these words from Proverbs. Commit whatever to the Lord, to the Mighty One of Israel, to our Abba Father. His shoulders are broad enough to take on all you do and make total success out of it all.

Even if the world expects you to be in control of your life, know that the one who really controls the world is waiting for you to turn it all over to him.

Prayer focus for today: Teachers in inner city schools.

OCTOBER 6

"What I feared has come upon me; what I dreaded has happened to me." (Job 3:25)

In any marriage, unless there's a set of unusual circumstances, one partner will be left alone. Maybe you used to wonder what would happen if *you* were the surviving spouse. How would you cope?

Well, here you are. What you feared and dreaded has happened. What is your reaction? Anger? Resignation? Guilt? Was Job's response the same as yours? He said that no matter what happened, he would still worship the God of the universe.

Another way of looking at this is to think of this contemporary slogan: "When life hands you lemons, make lemonade." If what you always dreaded would happen, *did* happen, look for the good that can come from it.

"What good?" you may ask. Look outside yourself and see who needs a helping hand. One of the greatest blessings the Lord gave me a few weeks after my husband died was being able to minister to a friend who desperately needed to talk about her problems.

Make lemonade!

Prayer focus for today: Students in Christian institutions of higher learning.

"Consider what great things he has done for you."
(1 Samuel 12:24)

An accepted practice in education is to give only positive comments first and then mention any negatives. This practice is especially useful in counseling students or in conferences with parents. It's easier to accept criticism or negative observations after focusing on what is good.

Could this be of help to us now at the potentially most negative time of our lives? It may be easier to think only of the bad things that have happened. It may even be more natural to focus on our grief. It may be automatic to be upset about what God has taken away from us.

And then we see these words from Samuel. Consider what great things he has done for you! Is that what we should do? Instead of focusing on what he has done *to* us, we should look at what he has done *for* us.

Positives first!

Prayer focus for today: Baby Christians who have just been born again.

OCTOBER 8

He will cover you with his feathers, and under his wings
you will find refuge. (Psalm 91:4)

"What does God look like?" asks the four-year-old. "Does he have wings like the angels do?" We tell the child, "No," and then find this verse in his Word telling us, "he will cover us with his feathers and his wings." What do we do with this seemingly inconsistent information?

Let's think about a newborn chick. All it can do is run around aimlessly and make feeble little peeping noises. This chick desperately needs to be under the protection and care of the mother hen. It needs to be sheltered and safe from the wiles of the world.

Our Savior promises to cover us with his precious blood when we truly put our faith in him. In his blood, we find refuge from the pitfalls of the world.

So, the Lord's care for us is *like* that of a mother hen. He gives us this word picture of how he cares for us because in the scheme of eternity, we are creatures who tend to run around aimlessly and make feeble noises.

Praise God for his knowledge of our situation and for giving us information we can assimilate!

Prayer focus for today: Those with mental illness in the family.

May he give you the desire of your heart and make all your plans succeed. (Psalm 20:4)

When first reading this verse, you might assume that it is telling us the Lord will grant your every little whim. Then how come he didn't give you the desire of your heart to keep your spouse from dying?

We need to look at these words again and consider them from another perspective. Maybe these words are telling us that *he will give you the desires.* In other words, he will put desires in your heart. He, the author of life, will make you want the things he knows are best for you. He will plant ideas in your heart, and you will declare that they were your own ideas!

When his desires for us are our desires, then all our plans will succeed. His knowledge of what is best for us is perfect.

Thank you, Lord, for making *your* desire *my* desire.

Prayer focus for today: Christian television stations.

OCTOBER 10

> *"Here I am! I stand at the door and knock. If anyone hears my voice and opens the door, I will come in."*
> (Revelation 3:20)

Jesus uses vivid word pictures to help us understand. What could be more specific than the vision of him knocking at the door? He wants to come in, but being the perfect gentleman that he is, he wants to be invited.

He declares, "Here I am," as he knocks. We frail little humans sputter, "Where are you, Lord, now that I need you?" And he's there all the time, waiting and knocking at our door. All we have to is open it.

Try to keep this picture in you mind. Make it part of your very being. The next time you are tempted to question, "Why? When? How come?" hear him say, "Here I am," and see him eager to come in.

Prayer focus for today: Those who lead worship at church services.

"Be still, and know that I am God." (Psalm 46:10)

One of the greatest strides modern technology has taken for us is the remote control for the television set. Isn't it easy just to sit there in the soft easy chair and flip channels? What a feeling! We are in command!

That power we feel with our remote control is nothing compared with the infinite greatness of God. He tells us to be still and watch.

He has charge of everything. It may seem like he uses some sort of ethereal remote control to run our lives, but our God is personal.

One definition of God is that everything is his. *We* are his. The situation we are in is his. Our future is his. He knows us. His total control over us is complete and trustworthy.

Prayer focus for today: Parents of missing children.

OCTOBER 12

"My soul glorifies the Lord and my spirit rejoices in God my Savior." (Luke 1:46–47)

Lord, my soul and my spirit are not joyful right now. The death of my spouse has left me totally devoid of all joy. I feel like the old song "I'll Never Smile Again."

And as long as I dwell on the sorrow, there will be no joy in my spirit. It will continue to crush my soul and push me farther into despair.

Is there an antidote for this? Look at the verse again. My soul *glorifies* the Lord. We are created to glorify our Creator God. It is only when we glorify him and rejoice in him that we are doing what we were meant to.

Since our purpose is to be joyful in the Lord, we should seek that at all times in spite of our circumstances. When you feel the worst and when the sorrow threatens to overtake you, shake off the dust of woe and concentrate on glorifying the Lord. You'll soon feel your very soul rejoicing.

Prayer focus for today: Those who need further education to help them earn enough to support their family.

OCTOBER 13

"I will grant peace in the land, and you will lie down and no one will make you afraid." (Leviticus 26:6)

During our times of bereavement the days can be filled with the daily routine of working, shopping, and dusting the furniture, anything to stay busy. But the nights seem endless.

You may hear noises you never heard before—creaks, rattles, and swooshes. You wonder what they are. Are they harmless or a threat?

You may wonder if you locked the door. So you get up and check. You go back to bed. Still you hear noises. You try to forget them.

Then you wonder, "What if I forgot to set the burglar alarm? What if the alarm doesn't go off? What if? What if? What if the sky is falling!"

The Lord tells us he will grant peace in the land. This means in *your* territory at this time. He also promised you will lie down and "not be afraid." Close your eyes and trust him to do what he said he would.

Prayer focus for today: Parents of children in private schools.

OCTOBER 14

Whom have I in heaven but you? And earth has nothing I desire besides you. (Psalm 73:25)

For years, I was part of a pair. I probably built my security on that. I may have even banked my identity on being half of a pair. Now that I'm no longer one of two, I find the situation unnerving, to say the least. I need equilibrium.

Lord, you have put me in a situation where I am alone. Or am I really alone? You remind me that you are there for me. You desire that I depend totally on you. From you comes my true security. From you alone I can draw my identity of being your precious child.

So you're asking me to put you in the number one spot in my life. This spot is where I should have put you all along. You tell me to seek first *you* and your Kingdom.

Forgive me, Lord, for failing to put you first. Starting with today, help me to put you in the rightful place.

Prayer focus for today: Those who are addicted to pornography.

O LORD, what is man that you care for him, the son of man that you think of him? (Psalm 144:3)

When I think of all the billions of people in your world, Lord, it "boggles" my mind to consider how you can care for each of them. Truly, you are magnificent. I stand in awe of you.

Of those billions, surely others are grieving as I am today. You assuredly are empathetic for them just as you are for me. How do you do it? I will never understand, but to you be the glory!

To you, let there be special glory and thanks for sending your Son to save each of those billions of people. Is this the secret of how your Son identifies with each of us weak little humans, because he became one of us?

The answer to the question, "What is man?" is that you know all about man because you made man. Man is the reason you sent your Son to be the perfect solution, to atone for man's shortcomings.

Prayer focus for today: Children who must grow up in inner cities.

OCTOBER 16

"Blessed is the man who will eat at the feast in the king-dom of God." (Luke 14:15)

One of the promises we are sure of is that there will be a great celebration feast when we come into Glory and meet our Lord face to face. He will welcome us with the wedding feast of the Lamb.

Notice we are promised in this verse, we *will* eat at the feast in the kingdom of God. This is future tense. It will happen sometime in the future.

But we don't have to wait for all the promises of God. Look at the verse again. Blessed is the man. This means we are blessed *now.*

If you're looking forward to joining your spouse in Heaven, that's wonderful. But you are blessed by the Lord now as well. Reach out to him and accept what he is offering. Seize the day!

Prayer focus for today: Mothers of elementary school children.

For a thousand years in your sight are like a day that has just gone by. (Psalm 90:4)

The future looms ahead of me like an unending path of uncertainty. I'm not looking forward to going on alone. I'm not sure I can do it. How long will I be alone?

Then you remind me that first, I am *not* alone. You're with me, carrying me through the days, weeks, months, years, however long my trek on this planet will be. You also remind me that a thousand years are as nothing in your sight. In my human, finite mind, I see years looming ahead. You, in your infinite perfect wisdom, see all this from the perspective of eternity.

Thank you, Lord, for reminding me of your assurance of eternity. Thank you for reminding me that my days on this earth are but a twinkling of an eye. Thank you, Lord, for your perfect timing that does not measure by day, week, month, or year, but forever!

Prayer focus for today: Nurses in home health care.

OCTOBER 18

And hope does not disappoint us. (Romans 5:5)

Your friends, your Christian brothers and sisters, rally around you when you lose a spouse. They cry with you and grieve along with you. They call just to check in. They invite you to dinner with them.

But sooner or later, it slows down. Someone says, "I'll call you tomorrow" and you get no call. You're disappointed. You really looked forward to their call.

Remember, dear child of God, in your grief you are more fragile than usual. Disappointments and setbacks seem far more crushing to you now.

Don't fall into Satan's snare of making you think that one disappointment means you'll be disappointed in everything. Don't let him even give you a twinge of thinking that the Lord will do the same.

We are promised that the Lord is with those who truly believe. He who lavishes hope upon us will never let us down.

So, praise him for always being with you. Accept the joy and hope he pours out on you.

Prayer focus for today: Those with a quarrelsome spirit.

Hear my prayer, O LORD; let my cry for help come to you. (Psalm 102:1)

I say, "Hear my prayer, O Lord," and then turn around and depend upon human or earthly resources. In theory I ask you for help with my finances and then I worry about how I'm going to pay the bills. Or, I ask you for peace and then fret and moan about being widowed.

Forgive me, Lord, for not trusting you to hear my cries for help. You've said you hear my prayers. That also means you pay attention to them. It also means that you are there to help. How dare I ask and immediately do my "human" thing to try to solve the problem?

My fervent prayer then, Lord, is for faith and trust. I know you will provide material things for me. Just grant me the measure of faith and trust that you know what I need.

Thank you, Lord!

Prayer focus for today: Those who are hearing impaired.

OCTOBER 20

*He will keep you strong to the end, so that you will
be blameless on the day of our Lord Jesus Christ.*
(1 Corinthians 1:8)

L ord, I'm so tired! These days of adjusting to my
new life wear me out. I feel far from strong. But
you're telling me that you will keep me strong to the
end. How?

And then you remind me that it's not for me to
know how you do it, just accept the fact that you
promised to do it. Do I need to know precisely how a
gasoline engine works to be able to drive a car? Do I
understand the aerodynamics of how a 747 flies? Does
my little grandson need to be able to calculate the
speed of a pitch as his daddy plays catch with him?

In the same way, it is enough for me to know that
if God promised to strengthen me, he *will do it.*

So, when I'm feeling weary with all the details of
what's going on right now in my life, I need to look to
the Mighty One of Israel whose promises never fail.

He will keep you and me strong to the end.

Prayer focus for today: Clients of Christian counseling
services.

We also rejoice in our sufferings, because we know that suffering produces perseverance; perseverance, character; and character, hope. (Romans 5:3–4)

Paul is telling us in these verses to rejoice in our sufferings. It may, at first, sound negative, but look, we're not left there in the pits of suffering or sorrow. Instead, we're shown that suffering is only the first building block.

It's a little like a kindergartner working with unit blocks. First one, then another, and so on until the final result is formed.

Maybe the Lord is using these words to remind us of why things are uncomfortable right now and that this is only the beginning of what will be. One block of suffering is the foundation for the next. The end result is something the Lord desires for you. That "something" is hope.

Just for today, keep focused on what the Lord hopes for you. Let him build in his infinitely wise way.

Prayer focus for today: Families of those who must travel frequently as part of their job.

OCTOBER 22

Praise be to God, who has not rejected my prayer or withheld his love for me! (Psalm 66:20)

You don't have to be in the world long to realize that it can be a hostile environment. In the vernacular, it's a "dog eat dog" world. This is often true when you are in business surroundings. It can also be true in other interpersonal situations. It's easy to feel rejected by others. You may feel unloved by those with whom you interact daily.

Today in your more-vulnerable-than-usual state, you may feel rejection more keenly. You may feel that no one cares about you or about your time of being left alone.

But there is one who never rejects you. This one gives you his love wholeheartedly. This one is the only one who really counts. This one is the Mighty One of Israel, our God.

Praise be to this Mighty One. He assures you that your prayers enter his throne room, the Holy of Holies, and he sends down showers of his love to you.

Prayer focus for today: Parents of children with learning disabilities.

OCTOBER 23

On him we have set our hope that he will continue to deliver us. (2 Corinthians 1:10)

Everybody is full of advice these days. Just look at the titles in the media. There are articles on "How to Make Your First Million Dollars." Editorials try to tell us how the world trade should be adjusted. Psychological gurus claim they can teach you inner peace.

Many of these modern ideas are in the same category as chasing rainbows. They may look good, but in the end, you don't find a pot of gold. What do you find? Disappointment.

Is there anything we can truly rely on? You know the answer to that question, dear child of God. The One who is worthy of our trust and hope is the Lord Jesus Christ.

No matter who or what we face, he alone is ready to deliver us. He never fails.

Prayer focus for today: Patients in shock trauma units.

OCTOBER 24

Cast your cares on the LORD and he will sustain you.
(Psalm 55:22)

Your cares create anxiety and worry in your soul. Worry has been defined as, "taking responsibilities God never intended you to carry." Right now, in the midst of your grief, why do you hold on to your cares?

The Lord is the strong one. The mighty God of the universe is there to pick up your worries, your cares, those responsibilities he intends to carry for you. He made this explicitly clear when he sent his only son to take the stripes on his back for you! One of those stripes on Jesus' back was specifically for you and your cares at this moment of your life.

So, don't do him the injustice of being unwilling to give them up. Instead, cast them all on him. With tears in your eyes, pile all that anxiety on his wounded, lacerated, but *perfect* back. And with his mighty power, he will sustain you.

Give him all the praise!

Prayer focus for today: Adoptive parents.

*He came and preached peace to you who were far away
and peace to those who were near.* (Ephesians 2:17)

When you fly in a big commercial jet, do you ever look down and see all the houses, cars, and trucks? From your perspective, they're all so small and yet there are so many of them. Each house, car, and truck contains so many people. As the plane flies and covers more and more territory, you see more and more people. Do you suppose God looks at his world from this perspective?

He tells us in his word that he cares for those who are far away and those who are near. That must mean *everybody*, those in little houses, those in big cities, those in Third World countries, everybody.

He cares for the everybodies and desires peace for all of them. His peace begins in the heart of each of us. So let us pray for his perfect peace to settle in our hearts today. May this blot out any feelings of fear, depression, or anger and help us focus totally on his blessings for those near and far.

Prayer focus for today: Volunteers for Meals on Wheels.

OCTOBER 26

Teach me to do your will, for you are my God.
(Psalm 143:10)

You know the cliché. When all else fails, follow the directions. At first, we may think this applies only in terms of putting together a new bookcase. But now, especially in this time of adjustment to being widowed, we do need guidance as we strive to put our lives together.

Do you read the manufacturer's directions before using a new item? Or do you go off on your own ingenuity and try to do it without reading them? The Lord tells us, read his directions.

When the Lord tells us this, we need to remember that he is our manufacturer. He made us and knows how we should operate. He gives us specific directions in his word.

The best way for us to learn the will of our God is to read his book faithfully. In searching out his directions every day, we will begin to see his will for our lives. Seeing this certainly puts daily events, even our sorrows, in the proper perspective.

Prayer focus for today: Men who exploit women.

In my anguish I cried to the LORD, and he answered by setting me free. (Psalm 118:5)

Picture how you feel when you're plodding through deep snow. You have to step high. Your legs get tired. You must be extremely careful not to slip and fall. It's tough going! You feel boxed in by the snow. You say, "Lord, help me!"

Then you come to a portion of the way that has been shoveled. Praise God! You can walk by simply putting one foot in front of the other. It's so much easier. Whoever shoveled that snow, in a sense, set you free.

Can you see the Lord in this picture? We mere mortals plod along fighting snow, muck, and pitfalls. Tough going! We say, "Lord, help us."

And he does! He provides some way to set us free, just as the shoveler of snow did.

He can set you free today from the cares that threaten to bog you down. He is eager to answer.

Just ask!

Prayer focus for today: Laypersons who are church leaders.

302

OCTOBER 28

"God will wipe away every tear from their eyes."
(Revelation 7:17)

In the book of Revelation, we are given many dramatic word pictures of what is to come. In chapter seven, we read about the great multitude in white robes. This multitude includes people from every tribe and nation. They all praise and sing to the Lamb of God. What a glorious time that will be!

The surroundings are a heavenly city so beautiful that we, in our less-than-perfect human form, cannot imagine the total splendor. But we're assured that it's there waiting for those who are born again and whose names are written in the Lamb's book of life.

The Lamb will wipe away every tear from our eyes. There will be no more sadness. Someone once suggested that God's jewels are crystallized tears. He will take our tears of sadness and make something beautiful of them.

Today, he wants to wipe away your tears. Cling to the promise and *let* him make them into jewels.

Prayer focus for today: Mothers of preschool children.

OCTOBER 29

I am greatly encouraged; in all our troubles my joy knows no bounds. (2 Corinthians 7:4)

There's an old, old story about a man hitting himself on the head with a rubber mallet. When asked why he was doing this, he replied, "It feels so good when I stop."

When you get past the absurdity of this story, one element of truth arises. You most appreciate feeling good after less pleasant circumstances. It's a little bit like having a headache and then getting relief by taking medication.

"Okay," you say, "that's an oversimplification. *My* troubles are greater than a headache caused by a rubber mallet."

You're right, dear child of God. Your troubles *are* greater than a mere headache. But look at the verse, "encouraged in *all* our troubles." That "all" encompasses your finances, your loneliness, your grief, whatever is troubling you at this time. We are to be encouraged in *all* of these.

Trusting in the one true God and turning over all our troubles to him will give us what he promised, joy that knows no bounds.

Thank you, Lord, for the troubles which in turn bring me boundless joy.

Prayer focus for today: Children with cystic fibrosis, and the research to find a cure.

OCTOBER 30

With you is the fountain of life. (Psalm 36:9)

Do you like maple syrup? I don't mean the artificially flavored stuff. What we're talking here is pure, undiluted maple syrup. Have you thought about where it comes from?

It comes from sugar maple trees. But it doesn't just "come" from those trees. It's waiting inside and has to be extracted or "tapped." A hollow tube is hammered into the tree. A pail or other receptacle is somehow added to the end of the tube. The tube must go deep enough to reach the sap. It is then that the collection process begins. The sap or syrup drips out into the pail. You might say that it is extracted from the source. It's a fountain of syrup.

The Lord is a little like that. He is the fountain of our life. He wants to provide for us. All we are called to do is tap into that fountain. His water is sweet and satisfying. It's there waiting for us.

Prayer focus for today: Christians who are under discrimination.

"As for me, I am in your hands; do with me whatever you think is good and right." (Jeremiah 26:14)

Before the modern miracle of instant tea, people used to make iced tea the old fashioned way. The scenario went something like this.

Boil the water. Put in the tea. Let it steep for a time. Remove the tea and strain the liquid. Add ice to cool it. Add sugar to sweeten it and lemon to give it a tang. What a process! Make it hot, make it cold, make it sweet, make it sour.

Maybe your life has been like that lately—hot, cold, sweet, sour. You may ask the Lord, "What are you doing with my life?" And then he reminds you, "You are in *my hands.*"

Of course, you're right, Lord. We are in your hands. And that implies that you must do whatever you know is good and best for us. If we feel we're being tossed about hot, cold, sweet, sour, remind us of that.

Praise you Lord!

Prayer focus for today: Blessings on those who give willingly to support the work of the Lord.

NOVEMBER I

It is God's will that you should be sanctified.
(1 Thessalonians 4:3)

As a marriage partner, you were in a physical relationship. Now that your spouse is dead, what
do you do about your sexual needs?

If you follow advice from the secular world, you
could get into habits of self-gratification. Psychological counselors of the world may tell you that
whatever feels good for you is all right. If that means
involvement with another person while you're single,
that's OK. You're an adult. You have your rights.

The advice that is best for all of us is found in
God's word. He tells us *it is his will that we be sanctified.*
Sanctification is the process of being made holy. Part
of seeking to be holy is to work daily to overcome
desires that are not of the Scriptures.

For example, we're told to clothe ourselves with
the Lord Jesus Christ. Each moment, each hour, each
day that you overcome those sexual urgings, you will
find the blessings of the Lord as he sanctifies you.

Prayer focus for today: Those running for public office.

"You will surely forget your trouble, recalling it only as waters gone by." (Job 11:16)

I enjoy sitting and watching a stream. It's calming to my soul. As the water rushes by, sometimes bubbling over stones, sometimes slowing into a small pool of quieter water, I'm certain the Lord created these miniature waterways for his children to receive the blessing of relaxation.

Sometimes a leaf floats by. I see it coming and then it is in full vision. It passes by and is gone. The waters continue to flow, but from where I sit, the leaf can't be seen again.

The Lord promises us that our troubles are like that. We may have seen them coming like the leaf we spotted before it got here, or our troubles may have come upon us suddenly like a leaf being blown down from an overhead tree. As the leaf passes by, we're aware of its presence. It may get stuck in a pool or eddy, but sooner or later, it will pass by.

We can praise our God for giving us word pictures assuring us of what he will do for us.

Prayer focus for today: Premature babies.

NOVEMBER 3

"Blessed are those who mourn, for they will be comfort-ed." (Matthew 5:4)

Do you feel blessed as a mourner? That's a little warped, don't you thinkk? Blessed? Hardly!

But let's look at mourning in your time of loss. Do we agree that our Lord God made everything, that he made you and understands you, that he therefore created your emotions? Is mourning part of those emotions?

If he, the mighty God of the universe, gave you the capability, he must expect that you will mourn sometimes. It's OK. You have your Abba Father's permission. You have our Father's blessing.

He will not leave you in this state for the rest of your life. He will allow it as long as necessary for you. And the end of the promise Jesus gives us in Matthew is that you "will be comforted."

No matter how difficult it may be, try to look for the blessing, knowing full well that his perfect comfort is part of the promise.

Prayer focus for today: Single mothers.

Again you will take up your tambourines and go out to dance with the joyful. (Jeremiah 31:4)

You may read these words and think they're not for you. You may feel that you'll never smile again, much less rejoice or dance. The Lord has promised in these words that you will rejoice and be glad.

Who wrote these words in our verse today? Jeremiah, who is best known as the prophet of doom. Scholars tell us that he was morose and full of self doubt.

Yet, this sorrowful person served the Lord and fulfilled what his Lord told him to do. His writings are full of things that the Lord is eager to tell his people.

So, when we read the words inspired by the Lord God and recorded by Jeremiah that we will be joyful, we can have the assurance that our God will carry us through these days and once again restore our joy.

Prayer focus for today: Those responsible for hiring and laying off personnel.

NOVEMBER 5

Many are the plans in a man's heart, but it is the LORD's purpose that prevails. (Proverbs 19:21)

L ord, we had so many plans for what we were going to do. First, we'd raise the kids, then we'd retire, then we'd travel, then . . . But those plans were cut off, and we didn't even have a vote in it.

What should I do now? Do you not want your children to think ahead? You cut off these plans my spouse and I made. Will you do the same if I plan to sell the house, or relocate, or change my career?

Then you remind me of the end of the story. It *is* your purpose that prevails. We in our human mind set many plans. You *do* honor our wishes, but, in the final analysis, what is best in your perfect eyes is what will be done.

Lord, thank you for showing me that. Help me to remember that as I plan ahead.

Prayer focus for today: Pray that voters will faithfully participate in elections.

His anointing teaches you about all things.
(1 John 2:27)

Have you ever had an eye-opening thought pop into your mind and wondered where it came from? Dear child of God, it came from the anointing that is within you as a believer. That anointing is the Holy Spirit given to you by the Holy One.

The Holy Spirit teaches us new things. But most of his teachings help us understand more about God. He shows us how to appreciate the *truth* that is God. It is when we allow this anointing to work within us that we are given insight into what he is so eager to share with us.

Today in this time of our bereavement, he is eager to comfort and share God's truth with us so we will understand his plan with more fullness.

Expect more eye-opening thoughts!

Prayer focus for today: Choir members.

NOVEMBER 7

"The LORD gave and the LORD has taken away; may the name of the LORD be praised." (Job 1:21)

The Lord gives. The Lord takes away. I've heard these words many times before, but they have a very intense meaning to me at this stage of my life. The Lord gave me my spouse. He gave me my marriage. He directed me in the path of living as a married person. Now, he's directing me down another path.

What if his choice for me had been no marriage at all? What if he had not led me to meet my spouse? What if he had chosen a totally single life for me? That could have been the path he had selected for me.

But he didn't. He gave me marriage and then he took it away. I need to look at the total picture. I need to be thankful for what I had for as long as I had it.

I need to praise the Name of the Lord!

Prayer focus for today: Parents of children confined to wheelchairs.

NOVEMBER 8

O my Strength, I sing praise to you; you, O God, are my fortress, my loving God. (Psalm 59:17)

Maybe you don't exactly feel like praising the Lord right now. You're still grieving. Maybe you're feeling a little guilty that you can't enter into an attitude of praise.

Dear child of God, be gentle with yourself. You are sad. You're going through a difficult time. Just remember what strength is available to you. Rest in him, that loving God.

And then, when you're ready once again to praise him, do it. Praise and sorrow cannot exist together. So, when you enter into an attitude of true praise, your grief will subside and then disappear.

Just for today, then, praise him. If you're alone, sing praises to him. Turn on a tape or tune in to a Christian radio station and join in corporate praise with others.

Prayer focus for today: Physicians who care for the elderly.

NOVEMBER 9

> *"It is not the healthy who need a doctor, but the sick.*
> *I have not come to call the righteous, but sinners."*
> (Mark 2:17)

Do you ever have guilt about the death of your spouse? "If only I had called the doctor sooner." "I should have recognized the signs." "I wish I had said kinder words." "If only I . . ."

Regrets . . . regrets . . . regrets. . .

Feeling guilt is OK; it's normal. Along with our other flaws, it demonstrates that we are not healthy, but need the perfection that is Jesus.

What a great teacher our Lord was! He drew such vivid word pictures that we can't help but understand what he's telling us. He came for those who need the doctor. He came for us poor sinners, not for the so-called righteous.

Aren't you glad that he did?

Prayer focus for today: Christian radio stations.

*"There is no one holy like the L*ORD*; there is no one besides you; there is no Rock like our God."* (1 Samuel 2:2)

Our God is a master teacher. He knows how slow we are to learn, so he uses all techniques to help us. He knows that at least we can understand what a rock is.

I love to picture the Lord as a rock. Solid. Dependable. Steady. These are all attributes possessed by our mighty God. He is a rock. He is not like sifting sand, changing with the wind. He is solid. We can cling to him.

As humans, we often try to cling to the little stones in our lives. Our possessions, our earthly relationships, and even our marriage are mere grains of sand when compared to the Rock.

The only true Solid Rock that will never change, of course, is our God.

So picture yourself holding on tightly to that Rock. Don't let the enticement of the world get in your way of grasping onto that.

Prayer focus for today: Those who harbor bitterness.

NOVEMBER 11

"So if the Son sets you free, you will be free indeed."
(John 8:36)

Once there was a parakeet named Beak. He lived in a nice little cage complete with bell, mirror, food dish, and water bottle. He had all the amenities a parakeet could want.

One day, Beak's owner moved his cage out into the driveway, so the cage could be cleaned. After the paper had been replaced and all the parakeet amenities were spotless, Beak's owner stood by to admire his work.

Beak looked at the latch on the door. It was ajar! Out of the cage Beak flew.

His owner was devastated. All the cries and pleas to come back went unheeded. Beak was free! But since Beak was a pet bird, he didn't know how to survive in the wild. In a short time, he fell prey to more savvy wild creatures.

Freedom is an exhilarating thing, making us feel invincible and reckless as the bird escaping the cage. The Master wants to free us from everything that prevents us from fulfilling our potential in Christ. But with this freedom comes responsiblities, disciplines and danger. Thank the Lord for your freedom in him, but use your freedom wisely. Freedom can turn into bondage, and bondage detains you from reaching the goal that God purposed for you.

Prayer focus for today: Blessings on those who read the Word daily.

NOVEMBER 12

Come quickly to me, O God. You are my help and my deliverer; O LORD, do not delay. (Psalm 70:5)

There's an expression, "Lord, I need patience— right now!" When I look at this verse from the Psalms, I think of that expression. The psalmist is asking God to come to his aid quickly without delay.

I must admit that many times I am impatient with God. I don't understand why my prayers are not answered right away. I prayed for him to heal my husband. His answer was to take him.

Then I am reminded that the Lord does answer prayer quickly. But his measurement of time and mine are not the same. His answers are always in his perfect time.

Thank you, Lord, for pointing out to me that you are eager to help me and to answer me quickly— in your time.

Prayer focus for today: Courage for those who fear.

NOVEMBER 13

We are not trying to please men but God, who tests our hearts. (1 Thessalonians 2:4)

We tell children to mind their manners. Newspaper columns give advice on proper courtesies to follow in dealing with people. We try not to talk with our mouths full. We almost always use the correct spoon at a dinner party. The purpose of manners is so that we won't offend anybody.

It's fine to consider others. Sometimes, however, we are unwilling to tell others about Jesus because we don't want to offend. There is one we should never offend. That One is the mighty God of Israel.

What can we do about this situation? Is there a way to witness without being offensive? God knows our hearts. He knows our abilities. He knows the words we need to speak to others. When we ask him for help, he will present the persons and situations to us and guide us through. He can use our bereaved situation effectively to accomplish this.

Thank you, Lord!

Prayer focus for today: Christian aerobic exercise programs.

NOVEMBER 14

"You are to be holy to me because I, the LORD, am holy, and I have set you apart from the nations to be my own." (Leviticus 20:26)

It seems that we humans thrive on having idols to look up to. We admire television personalities. We cheer our favorite sports figures. We even model our lives on what we see and admire in others.

If those we are modeling are born-again believers, we can learn a lot from watching them. On the other hand, if the observed values of our idols are not of the Lord, we would be well advised to sit back and remember to whom we belong.

The model we should admire and seek is our Holy God. He tells us to be holy because he is holy. We may realize we're far from being that. But we can learn how to become closer by daily seeking the face of the Lord. When we daily have devotions, read the Scriptures, and pray, we are seeking his face.

If the world doesn't understand your habits, it's all right. They may look at you now and think this is all part of your mourning. Just keep up the quest for holiness now and for the rest of your days here on earth.

Prayer focus for today: Emergency room personnel.

NOVEMBER 15

*"I will strengthen you and help you; I will uphold you
with my righteous right hand."* (Isaiah 41:10)

I have a set of wind chimes hanging on the screened
lanai at my home. It's really quite pleasant to be
in the house and hear the chimes as they move gently with the billows of breezes. When I'm outside
and hear them, I look up. They move, but the vehicle
for moving them is invisible.

Though the wind itself cannot be seen, the
actions caused by the wind can. Our Lord and his
providential care are much like that. He tells us he
will uphold us with his righteous right hand. To my
knowledge, few people have actually seen God's hand
holding them up. But many of his saints feel him
holding them and keeping them up out of the mire
of this world.

Today as you continue to live in your new status
of singleness, feeling his hand holding you up is
probably more important than ever. Just lean back,
close your eyes, and pretend *you* are a wind chime.

Prayer focus for today: Parents of children who are visually impaired.

For the LORD God is a sun and shield; the LORD bestows favor and honor; no good thing does he withhold from those whose walk is blameless. (Psalm 84:11)

Our Lord is often referred to as a bright light. Under a bright light, all our imperfections show up, some we didn't even know we had: "Is my hair really getting that gray? I didn't realize my hands were that wrinkled." The light shows us how we *really* are.

And yet our Lord wants our walk with him to be blameless. How can we ever aspire to that when we know that his brilliant light is shining on us, showing all our flaws?

The answer, dear child of God, is that he is not only a sun, but also a shield. He needs to point out our imperfections, but he is also there as our defender and protector.

He understands perfectly. His light shows when we feel angry about being bereaved. Yet he wraps his arms around us at the same time and loves us with an everlasting love.

Prayer focus for today: Blended families.

NOVEMBER 17

Praise be to the God and Father of our Lord Jesus Christ.
. . .who comforts us in all our troubles.
(2 Corinthians 1:3–4)

When we see the purple mountain majesties with the sun shining down, brightly splashing on the iridescent petals of honeysuckle, our hearts burst with praise for the mighty God who created all this and more. Wow! Praise him!

It may be more difficult to think of praising him when your marriage has been cut off by death. But we are called to be a praising people.

Even though you don't feel like it, praise him. You can't trust your feelings. Praise him anyway. Start your day with it. Do it as you go through the day. Praise him with your voice and with your heart.

Before you know it, you'll be comforted. We're promised that God himself is there to comfort us in *all* our troubles.

Praise him!

Prayer focus for today: Those who enforce the law in urban areas.

*The LORD watches over the alien and sustains the father-
less and the widow.* (Psalm 146:9)

Two years after my husband died, I moved to
another state. This meant new living arrangements, learning where to shop, changing my driver's
license, and all the other adjustments that go along
with moving to a new area. It also meant finding a
new place of worship.

I found the church where I thought the Lord
wanted me to be. It had a singles department. So, I
became part of it and attended many of their social
functions.

Since I felt a little like an alien, I didn't talk about
the specifics of my single situation. One day, however, I was asked directly about my marital status. After
I explained that I am a widow, one of the singles said,
"Oh, I just assumed you were divorced." Another
said, "I figured you ditched your husband."

This is sad commentary to me on how we view
others we don't know. We can't assume or prejudge
others. We should be gentle with them. In this way,
we can be of assistance to the Lord as he watches
over the alien, the fatherless, and the widowed.

Prayer focus for today: Bible study groups.

NOVEMBER 19

> *So whether you eat or drink or whatever you do, do it all for the glory of God.* (1 Corinthians 10:31)

Today people are highly conscious of health and fitness. They are concerned with what they eat and drink. Fat content is advertised on everything, even fast food! People are concerned about general health, so exercise regimens are in.

We need to analyze this fetish for health. Why do we watch our foods and keep up with our exercise? To look good? To feel well? To live longer?

Those are all good reasons for caring for our bodies. But there's a deeper reason why we should do these things.

If we recall that the chief purpose of humans is to glorify God and enjoy him forever, then we will see a glimmer of what Paul is telling us in today's verse. Whatever we do, we should do it to glorify God.

Easy to say! Especially when our circumstances are doldrums not of our choosing. But when we concentrate solely on glorifying God, then whatever we do will point us toward God and out of our doldrums!

Prayer focus for today: Those caring for patients in mental hospitals.

I will sing with my spirit, but I will also sing with my mind. (1 Corinthians 14:15)

We sing praises to the Lord. Our voices join together in a chorus of worshipping the God of the universe. When we do this, we can feel the choir of those who have gone ahead of us into heaven, joining with our hymn of adoration. Maybe we can almost hear the voices of our spouses as they sing hallelujah to the Lamb of God.

We can also sing when we're by ourselves. Whether our voices are opera quality or shower quality doesn't matter. When we think only of our God and all he's done for us, his praise will be on our lips.

Paul suggests that we sing with our "spirit" and sing with our "mind." Singing with the spirit is the practice that brings us closer to him. Singing with our mind is a more willful activity. It includes making a concerted effort to sing to him no matter what circumstances we are in.

So make it a practice to sing to the Lord in corporate worship and sing to him when you're alone.

Prayer focus for today: Single mothers who give up their babies for adoption.

NOVEMBER 21

*"Therefore come out from them and be separate," says the
Lord.* (2 Corinthians 6:17)

I often think of media presentations on television
and in motion pictures. Things I would have been
shocked at ten years ago, now barely phase me. I have
been numbed to it by accepting the values of the world.

The Lord tells us to be separate. He wants us to
be "in" the world. How else could we be a witness for
him. But he does not want us to be "of" the world.
He calls us to holiness in him.

Today in this time of our adjusting to being alone,
the world may seem more appealing than ever. We are
in a fragile state, so we must be wary of that which
threatens to corrupt us.

Our solution is to follow our Savior's directive to
be separate in our thinking and separate in our actions.
Be separate from the world, but be one with him!

Prayer focus for today: Blessings on those who revile you.

They will be like a well-watered garden, and they will sorrow no more. (Jeremiah 31:12)

This is the time of year when Christmas Trees for Sale signs begin to appear. Christmas trees come in a variety of species and sizes. They're imported from far away states and they are grown nearby. You can even go to a choose-and-cut lot for your Christmas tree.

Many trees have a lovely conical shape. They look so nice and uniform in those rows of trees. But, you know what? They don't grow that way all by themselves. They have to be sheared. This process is a real art and takes place during the hot summer months. Many growers use long knives and shears. Others use mechanical devices.

When the trees are first sheared, they look a little shabby. But this is necessary to produce a tree with the sought-after shape of a Christmas tree.

The Lord sometimes finds it necessary to "shear" our lives. It is his choice to do what he must to shape us into what he seeks after in us. We may grieve as he shapes us. But our current status of being single may be part of his process of shaping us.

Prayer focus for today: Those who staff stores that are open all night.

NOVEMBER 23
> *"The spirit is willing, but the body is weak."*
> (Mark 14:38)

You notice your clothes are getting a little tight. Time to go on a diet! You really will do it this time. You start off with great resolve, and it lasts, until that piece of chocolate cake comes along. You can figure out the end of this story. The spirit is willing, but *oh the chocolate cake!*

Maybe in your grieving and adjusting process you have a willing spirit but feet of clay. Maybe you really want to do better, but those uncontrollable tears keep falling. "I should do better," you say.

Dear child, don't be so hard on yourself. You've been through a trauma. All the resolve in the world won't change that.

If you need to cry, allow yourself. If you feel you are doing better and then those pangs of sorrow overflow, don't feel like you're a failure. Instead, rejoice that you are human, as the Lord made you.

Be patient with your feet of clay. Sooner or later they will catch up with your spirit!

Prayer focus for today: Those who have lost their job.

My days are like the evening shadow; I wither away like grass. (Psalm 102:11)

Since my husband died, I often feel like I should just go and hide in the shadows. I wish I could see no one. I wish no one could see me. I feel like withered grass—dried up and undesirable. It's easy to feel sorry for myself when I let those feelings have control of me.

It is at those times that I need to remind myself I can't go by my feelings. They're not reliable gauges of my true worth. My value is that I am a child of the Most High Father. I am lovely in his sight, no matter how I feel I look.

So what I have to force myself to do, then, is take better care of my physical appearance. I splash water on my face to get rid of the tears. I go to my closet and pick out the most attractive outfit I own. I brush my hair and put on fresh makeup.

Then I look in the mirror and remind myself, I am a daughter of the King! I go out from the shadows and into the world to be the best representative of him I can be.

Prayer focus for today: Grandparents who are raising their grandchildren.

NOVEMBER 25

"Now is your time of grief, but I will see you again and you will rejoice, and no one will take away your joy."
(John 16:22)

Just imagine how the disciples must have felt when Jesus told them now was their time of grief. He let them know ahead of time that hard times were coming.

Sound like your life? In your time of grief, have you asked, "Why?"

The Lord told his disciples that he would see them again which would cause them to rejoice greatly.

Sound like what you hope your life will be like?

We're promised that we'll see our loved ones again. What joy that will be! It will be something no one can take away. There will be no more sorrow, no more separation, just basking in the pure joy of being with our loved ones where we will praise the Risen Lamb for all eternity!

Prayer focus for today: Patients in intensive care units.

NOVEMBER 26

The LORD is near to all who call on him, to all who call on him in truth. (Psalm 145:18)

Now that I am widowed, I seem to notice how alone I really am. Before, I thought nothing of going to a movie by myself. Now I do. I am painfully aware of all those who are there with their spouses. They are two. I am one. I am alone.

But the Lord tells me I'm not really alone. He assures me that he is near to all who call on him. I've been so occupied with feeling sorry for myself that I haven't called on him, the one who's always there, who will never be called away from me.

So from now on, I will resolve to call on him more often. When I see couples, I will call on the Lord for solace. When I fear the future, I'll reach out to him. When I feel nothing, I will call on him.

And I will rejoice that I am in this situation where I am called to need him moment by moment.

Prayer focus for today: Those who use their gift of mercy.

NOVEMBER 27

May the God of hope fill you with all joy and peace as you trust in him. (Romans 15:13)

Maybe today you aren't exactly overflowing with joy and peace. Maybe the details of adjusting to your new state of singleness are claiming your attention. What can you do about it?

First, you need to look at this verse and what it has to say. Our God is not a God of sorrow. He weeps far more than we do in our hour of grief. Rather, our God is a God of hope.

Hope can also be thought of as confidence, safety, and trust. In other words, dear child of God, seek our Lord and trust him. Have confidence that he cares for you more than you could ever imagine. Seek him and know with certainty that you are safe with him.

As you focus on trusting him, you will soon feel his joy and peace cascading over you. Savor this sensation. Soak it up. Let it become part of your being. It's the greatest antidote for grief there is.

Prayer focus for today: Christians who daily seek the Lord.

NOVEMBER 28

"Before I formed you in the womb I knew you, before you were born I set you apart." (Jeremiah 1:5)

The prospective mother has juvenile onset diabetes. On one of her first visits to the medical experts, it was determined that her blood sugars had been out of control when she unexpectedly became pregnant. The experts hinted that it may be wise to terminate the pregnancy. But the mother is a child of the King. She said *that* would not be an option. So the pregnancy continued.

Other experts suggested that since the blood sugars were high, the baby's heart could be damaged. Still the mother held to her convictions.

The next week, a prophecy was given during a worship service. The prophet saw Jesus standing between doctors and an unborn child. The doctors said that the baby's heart is damaged. Jesus said it was all right because, "I am the healer." Those who are near to this mother claimed the promise for her and her child.

The pregnancy continued to completion. The child is beautiful! Her heart is perfect. She is a true blessing from the Lord. This is only one of many blessings our Lord has for those who carry his name.

Look for what he's waiting to bless you with!

Prayer focus for today: Church nursery workers.

334

NOVEMBER 29

"I am the bread of life. He who comes to me will never go hungry, and he who believes in me will never be thirsty." (John 6:35)

What a master of understanding our Lord is! He is an expert on human needs and comprehension. He uses vivid word pictures to describe his role in our salvation. He knows that we mortals are hungry and thirsty. He uses this knowledge to show us how completely he can fill all our needs.

Maybe you're hungry and thirsty for peace today. All the human things you've tried just don't do it. You may have read secular books filled with platitudes on grieving. You may even have sought a therapist to help you get real with your emotions. Still hungry and thirsty?

Then go to the one who understands completely. He offered himself to be food and drink for our souls. He told us that when we come to him, we'll never be hungry or thirsty again. In him is your perfect peace, your perfect acceptance of where you are today, and your perfect satisfaction and comfort.

Prayer focus for today: Those who are paralyzed.

And whatever you do, whether in word or deed, do it all in the name of the Lord Jesus, giving thanks to God the Father. (Colossians 3:17)

Look at the calendar. Do you know there are only twenty-four shopping days until Christmas? Or don't you care this year? The stores try to entice us so we will be swept away with buying. Is it hard for you right now? Has your bereavement robbed you of the joy you used to have in getting ready for Christmas?

There is a solution. We're told by Paul that whatever we do should be done in the name of the Lord. If we focus our attention on him and what would please him, we won't get swept away by the frenzy of the Christmas shopping season.

Christmas, after all, is the time we have chosen to commemorate the birth of our Savior. However we celebrate it, our major focus should be on him and what he has done for us by saving us.

Prayer focus for today: Students Against Drunk Driving (SADD).

DECEMBER 1

When he appears, we shall be like him, for we shall see him as he is. (1 John 3:2)

Many of us need corrective lenses to be able to see things more clearly. We use bifocals, reading glasses, or contact lenses to help us bring into focus what we see. This is good and a blessing from our Lord to give us needed assistance while we're in this world.

But he promises us that when he appears, when he comes again, we shall see him as he is. We can't really see him now, but when he returns again, we'll know him as he is. And he says we shall be like him.

When we're made like him, we can throw away those corrective lenses. We'll see him clearly. When we are like him, we won't feel sorrow anymore. We can throw away our box of tissues. When we are like him, we will see, sense, and feel the world in a state of his perfection.

Come, Lord Jesus!

Prayer focus for today: Medical personnel who work in trauma centers.

DECEMBER 2

*Do not hide your face from your servant; answer me
quickly, for I am in trouble. Come near and rescue me.*
(Psalm 69:17–18)

Where are you, God? Tragedy, bereavement, and
trouble have struck, and I feel you're hiding
your face from me. I've tried to be your servant. Where
are you? Please come near to me now.

Does this mean God has moved? Is he deliber-
ately in hiding? Or is God the unchanging one and
I'm the one who moved?

His Word tells me that he is the same yesterday
and today. So he must still be there. Maybe I have let
my sorrow get in the way, and it is my own sorrow
that hides his face from me.

So I resolve now, for today, to seek the Lord with
all my heart, to lay aside dependency on grief, and
to let him come to me and remove me from my own
negative emotions.

Praise him for being so near!

Prayer focus for today: Those who need to relocate due
to job change.

DECEMBER 3

*And we know that in all things God works for the good
of those who love him, who have been called according to
his purpose.* (Romans 8:28)

Lord, I know you tell me that in *all* things you work for good. But it's so hard to accept that right now in my time of deflated joy.

Then I need to look beyond and focus on the rest of these inspired words of Romans 8:28. You work for the good of those who love you.

I *do* love you, Lord, and I'm trying to focus on that. I'm trying to remember that all this is for good. Forgive me if I don't agree with this every second of every day. I'm trying.

You remind me that you've called me according to your purpose. You have an ultimate design in mind for why you have allowed these events in my life. Lord, please help me to never forget that and to give you all the glory.

Prayer focus for today: Nursing home residents.

He put a new song in my mouth, a hymn of praise to our God. (Psalm 40:3)

Ever been part of a group that's taught a new song or a new praise chorus and you think, "What's wrong with 'Rock of Ages' or even 'Jesus Loves Me'? Who needs to learn a new song?"

Dear child of God, you need to learn a new song. And learning something new implies a little bit of work on your part. The Lord will put a new song in your heart. Just listen and follow him, and before you know it, that new song is part of you.

He chooses to put that new song in you to prevent your clinging to the old, to the past. It's not that the old and the past are no good. They are your history. But the Lord knows you so well. He knows your need to learn a new song.

When you let it become part of your being, you soon will see that it is a hymn of praise. The Lord teaches you so that you are free to praise him. Sorrow and praise do not exist well together.

Praise the Lord with all your new songs!

Prayer focus for today: Blessings on those who tithe.

DECEMBER 5

We know that just as you share in our sufferings, so also you share in our comfort. (2 Corinthians 1:7)

The Lord healed me of my migraine headaches by using medical persons to teach me the probable causes of them. Before this, I really suffered. First would come the aura, a blinding light similar to a flash bulb shining in my eyes. I couldn't see except for a tiny periphery outside of that blinding light.

Next were the zigzag lights that flashed across my vision. Still I couldn't see well. And then came the excruciating pain of the actual headache which lasted for several hours.

Afterward, I would thank the Lord that once again, I could see. What relief! But had I not suffered so much, I may not have felt or appreciated that ultimate soothing.

We are called to walk with our brothers and sisters through their sufferings. In this way, we will share in their comforting. Others have walked these paths with us. It is our joy to respond by doing for them.

Prayer focus for today: Crisis pregnancy centers.

DECEMBER 6

Each heart knows its own bitterness, and no one else can share its joy. (Proverbs 14:10)

There is an old song, "Laughing on the Outside, Crying on the Inside." Maybe that's the way you feel today. You're trying to be strong, trying to show that you are adjusting, accepting, getting along in your bereaved situation.

Friends and acquaintances say you're doing so well. But you know how you feel. You try, but the serenity may be only skin-deep.

As this verse tells us, each heart knows its own sorrows. But the verse continues, each heart also experiences joy that only you can know. What joy could that be? It's the joy of knowing whose child you are. You are the most precious child in the world to him. If you were the only person in the world, Jesus still would have died to save *you.*

So let your heart bubble with the joy of knowing how deeply you are loved by the Mighty God of Israel.

Prayer focus for today: Children who are visually impaired.

DECEMBER 7

Do not be anxious about anything, but in everything, by prayer and petition, with thanksgiving, present your requests to God. (Philippians 4:5)

Have you ever observed a toddler's response to a jack-in-the-box? The child turns the handle, the little tune plays, and then out of the box jumps the jack! Jack is usually a white face clown with an oozy, smiling face. He bobs his curly, wigged head.

What are some of the responses to this from toddlers? Some squeal with delight as they await to see what's happening. Others wait with fear and anxiety. They may even cover their eyes and try to blot out what they fear will happen.

Through many experiences in our lives, we can be like the toddler who awaits with anxiety. We are concerned. We are afraid. We are anxious. But we are told not to be anxious about anything. The prescription our Lord gives us for this is to pray and give thanks in everything.

This includes our good times and our less-than-good times. Everything includes the days of our grief. He is more than sufficient to take away any anxiety and replace it with his perfect peace.

Prayer focus today: Those whose trust has been shattered.

"Forgetting what is behind and straining toward what is ahead, I press on toward the goal to win the prize for which God has called me." (Philippians 3:13–14)

Refrigerator magnets are popular right now. You see displays of them everywhere. Some are in the shapes of little animals. Others serve as photo frames, clips, and even note pads. I suppose the purpose of many of these magnets is to make a statement or to remind us of something.

May I suggest that you write the verse for today on a card and attach it magnetically to your refrigerator? Look at that verse. We're told to forget what is behind and work toward what God has in store for us.

It's not that we're told to forget our spouses. We're told to think of that time as what was. Now we are called to new goals he has planned for us.

Maybe those goals are to read the Word more, to study it more in depth. Maybe he wants you to commit to memory parts of the Word. Maybe he is waiting for you to spend more time talking to him in prayer. He does have specific goals just for you.

Whether you memorize this verse or put it on your refrigerator, let its words become part of you.

Prayer focus for today: Producers of television shows for children.

DECEMBER 9

How great is the love the Father has lavished on us, that
we should be called children of God! (1 John 3:1)

Our society is obsessed with love. Television shows
are bursting with it. Advertisers use romance to
sell cars, perfume, and even blue jeans. Magazine
articles tell us how to keep our love vibrant. It's nauseating! And it's especially nauseating to those of us
who are trying to adjust to being single again.

When I see advertisements or other media reminders of love, I frequently have to bite my lip to
keep from letting the tears flow. Will I always feel
this way?

Then the Lord reminds me of his great love for
me. This is not an earthly, sensual love. It is a pure,
flawless love he lavishes on me. With this love, he
completely understands me. This love is eternal.
Because of this love, I am a child of God. Hallelujah!

Thank you, Lord, for raising me up to your abid-
ing love.

Prayer focus for today: Sufferers of arthritis.

*My eyes stay open through the watches of the night, that
I may meditate on your promises.* (Psalm 119:148)

Nighttime. It's quiet and I'm alone. Everything is
silent except for the tick-tick-tick of the clock.
I hear the clock and the ticking, the hours chime,
and still I am awake. Hours pass, groups of hours
pass, and the night continues.

The ancient Hebrews divided the twelve hours of
their night into three segments with sets of guards
for each watch of the night. As I lie awake, I wonder
why. I never signed up to be one of the watchmen of
the night.

Then the Lord says to me, "My promise to you,
my precious child, is that you are special, and I will
continue to care for you even in the midst of your
bereavement and during your sleepless watches of the
night."

So, I am content in my sleeplessness during the
night. The quiet gives me time to meditate on the
Lord and what he says to me. Throughout the watches of the night, my soul is comforted.

Prayer focus for today: Business personnel who may be
tempted to deal dishonestly.

DECEMBER 11
"I have loved you with an everlasting love."
(Jeremiah 31:3)

Those convenience stores that are open twenty-four hours are really a welcome addition to our culture. Just think of it. If you want a frosty soda at 2:00 A.M, you can go get it. If you get hungry at 11:00 P.M. submarine sandwiches are available. Suppose you feel you need a crossword puzzle book at 4:00 A.M. You've got it! It's great to have access to a place that never closes and that is always there when you need something.

Does this remind you of someone? Our God has told us that his love for us is everlasting. This is not a nine-to-five love; it is a twenty-four hour love. It is never-ending!

Think what this means. We can approach him anytime. No matter what, he loves us. Even if we are angry that he chose to take our spouse, he still loves us. Even when we choose not to talk to him through prayer, he still loves us. He's waiting for us to realize how deep his love for us is. He's waiting to show us.

When we go to be with him, what everlasting joy we will know as we spend eternity basking in his everlasting love!

Prayer focus for today: Those undergoing psychiatric counseling.

DECEMBER 12

Therefore encourage one another and build each other up.
(1 Thessalonians 5:11)

When you find yourself widowed, it's easy to think you're the only one in the world who is in this situation. It's probably natural to feel this way, since you are still in shock with the finality of it.

As the days and weeks go by, you may find others who are alone. If statistics interest you, you may want to delve into census information at your local public library. You'll probably be surprised to find there are 13.9 million widowed persons in this country alone. Dear child of God, we are not the only persons who have endured the loss of a spouse.

The best human source of comfort I have found is being with others who have been widowed. Just talking about our mutual experiences and concerns is consoling to me. May I suggest that you find a support group? If you can't find one, then start one!

We are told to encourage one another and build each other up. This is particularly valuable for those of us who are walking this path of grief.

I encourage you to find others who will walk your path with you.

Prayer focus for today: Single fathers.

DECEMBER 13

The LORD will indeed give what is good, and our land will yield its harvest. (Psalm 85:12)

We may all agree that the Lord will give what is good. However, at this particular time of our lives, we may challenge that. What is good about being widowed? We may see only negatives in this.

The word "negative" is used in photography. What is a negative? It is the reverse of the picture that was taken. The light and dark parts are the opposite of what really is.

This negative can be used to make a print which will show things in a way we can see as "positive." This same negative, then, has the potential for becoming positive. It's all a matter of perspective.

Is it possible that the "negatives" in our life have potential for becoming "positive"?

Dear child of God, you probably have figured out by now that the answer is "yes."

It's all a matter of perspective.

Prayer focus for today: Youth pastors.

The old has gone, the new has come!
(2 Corinthians 5:17)

It's gone. My life as I knew it is no more. It's over. There's nothing to look forward to.

And then the Lord reminds me, "As long as you cling to the past, you will not forget it's gone. You will be down."

It's a lot like when I was first saved. The old me was gone, the stupid mistakes wiped out by the perfect Blood of the Lamb. Praise God the old has gone!

In its place is the new, a new outlook on life, a new promise of what will be. And so it can be with us now in the time of our adjustment to life without our spouse.

That life we knew and were comfortable with is no more. But rather than dwelling on that and lamenting what is no more, we need to be as content as possible with what is and look ahead to what will be.

Prayer focus for today: Grandparents.

DECEMBER 15

His divine power has given us everything we need for life and godliness. (2 Peter 1:3)

Do you make shopping lists? Experts tell us that we can do the most efficient shopping when we make a list and organize it according to the layout of the store. By using this system, supposedly we will remember everything we need.

But there are things in life and beyond that we don't need lists for. With his divine power, our God knows our needs even before we list them. If he actually had asked us to enumerate our wishes, we'd find that he gives us far more than what we ever could have thought of on our own. Yet we still question why he gave us, or took away, what or who we wish we had.

Our role today is to wait and see everything he is so willing to give us. We need to rest in his divine power and know that what he gives us or takes away is all we need for life and godliness.

Prayer focus for today: Unwed pregnant teen-age girls.

DECEMBER 16

With God we will gain the victory, and he will trample down our enemies. (Psalm 60:12)

What are your enemies during this time of being left alone? Self-pity? Anger? Loneliness? Fear? Do your numerous enemies loom and threaten to overtake you?

The children of Israel faced numerous enemies: idol-worshipping pagans who did not recognize the One True God, Jehovah. To the children of Israel, many of these enemies appeared to be gigantic—the Nephilim of Genesis. They were so large that when compared with them, the children of Israel felt like mere grasshoppers.

But what happened when the whole story was told? Who prevailed? The enemies or the One True God?

Just as the victory was won by the children of Israel, so you have victory. You have *complete victory* in Jesus. He will trample down those enemies that haunt you, even anger, self-pity, and loneliness.

Praise the God who is more than sufficient to make us victorious.

Prayer focus for today: Former mental patients who are now homeless.

DECEMBER 17

Life will be brighter than noonday, and darkness will become like morning. (Job 11:17)

Flying can be an exciting adventure. It's especially dramatic on a cloudy, overcast day. When your plane begins to ascend into the clouds, you may feel a little disoriented because of the fog surrounding you. But then, you're through the clouds and into full, dazzling sunlight. What a joy! What a change from the cloudy fog you were in previously.

Do you feel you're in a cloudy overcast condition at this time of your life? Losing a spouse can thrust you into the crater of despair where all you see are dim clouds.

Even when you try to pull yourself up and out of that abyss, you may feel disoriented, much as you did when the plane was going through the clouds. Readjusting one's life after being widowed can daze and bewilder you.

But keep on trying, and before you know it, you'll be through the clouds of your life. It is then you will be in the full gleaming brilliance of the presence of the Lord.

Prayer focus for today: Support groups for the widowed.

"For the foundations of the earth are the LORD's; upon them he has set the world. He will guard the feet of his saints." (1 Samuel 2:8–9)

I f you've ever built a house, you may remember seeing the foundation laid. It may have been a gigantic concrete slab. It may have been a series of cement blocks. It may have been basement walls upon which your house was anchored. Whatever form it took, we can all agree that the house is only as strong as its foundation.

Our world is like that, too. It is not literally set upon a cement block structure. Rather, our world is set firmly on the foundation established by the great God of the universe.

He assures us that he carefully has set the world on his foundation. In this perfect security, he promises us, his saints, that he will protect us and guard the ways we go.

So even if you are unsure of your footing in the midst of your sorrow, rest in his assurance. Be sure of his foundation. Trust him to guide you in the way he has chosen for you, even before the foundation of the world.

Prayer focus for today: Honesty in business.

DECEMBER 19

You are no longer foreigners and aliens, but fellow citizens with God's people and members of God's household. (Ephesians 2:19)

In our modern society, few people live near their extended families. Many people have to relocate often. Transfers are common. Changing professions and moving across the country are everyday occurrences. We are scattered and away from our blood relatives.

As we settle into a new community, our accents or mannerisms may be indicators that we are not native to that area. We may say, "I'm not from here."

In fact, we who know Jesus Christ as Savior are "not from here" either. Our Lord said his Kingdom is not of this world. Since we are King's Kids, we too are not from this world. We have a home in glory. Hallelujah!

What does that mean to us right now? The cares, the sorrows, the griefs of this world are nothing compared with what he has waiting for us.

Be glad you're not from here.

Prayer focus for today: Medical personnel in physicians' offices.

DECEMBER 20

*For the L*ORD *your God is God of gods and Lord of lords, the great God, mighty and awesome, who shows no partiality and accepts no bribes. He defends the cause of the fatherless and the widow.* (Deuteronomy 10:17–18)

Everybody has advice for the newly widowed. They swarm around you with suggestions on where to invest the insurance money or what agent to use to sell your house. Their eagerness and their supposed expertise are red flags of warning. Beware the Ides of Widowhood.

What's the answer? We need to seek wise counsel. We shouldn't jump at the first financial opportunity that appears. We need to take time. We need to ask advice from Spirit-filled financial experts. Then we need to sit back and think some more.

Our premier advice-giver is the Lord Jesus Christ. He is there for us. We need to speak with him in fervent prayer. He promises to defend our cause.

Prayer focus for today: Pray for producers of motion pictures.

DECEMBER 21

> *"Whoever humbles himself like this child is the greatest
> in the kingdom of heaven."* (Matthew 18:4)

Believe it or not, teaching children of preschool age can be a real balm to the ego. Those little ones look up to you with such awe.

They listen intently as you read a story to them. Anything the teacher says *has* to be true. They run up to you and hug your knees as they look up to you, their heroine. They feel safe and secure with you.

That's the way the Lord wants us to perceive him. He wants us to listen intently to him and believe what he has to say to us.

Even when you're missing your spouse, or maybe *because* you are missing your spouse, humble yourself as a child. Come to Jesus, the Lord of the Universe. Revel in his love and feel his perfect safety and perfect security.

Prayer focus today: Those who are tempted to shoplift.

For the LORD will not reject his people; he will never for-sake his inheritance. (Psalm 94:14)

There's an interesting phenomenon that frequently happens when you lose a spouse. People stand back and watch you in a state of something like awe. They may even ask, "How do you do it?" They look at you with pity. Note that they do all this from a safe distance.

You see, it seems that if they get too close, your experience may rub off on them. They act as if rubbing elbows with you in your bereavement may cause them to lose their spouse, too. It may remind them of their own mortality. Knowingly or unknowingly, they avoid you just because. They may say they don't know what to say. They, in their anxiety, are rejecting you. And it hurts, doesn't it?

It is especially vital at times like these for you to remind yourself of what the Lord is telling you in this psalm. He will *never* reject you. He understands your fragile feelings and he understands those who are reluctant to interact with you.

Our role, then, is to rest in his love and to pray for those who are not that blessed.

Prayer focus for today: Parents of stillborn babies.

DECEMBER 23

During the night an angel of the Lord opened the doors of the jail and brought them out. (Acts 5:19)

The "them" in this verse from Acts are apostles. Those in charge of them were envious of their miraculous deeds and put them in jail. At that time, the court system did not consider people to be innocent until proven guilty. Rather, it was the other way around. Talk about injustice!

But what happened? The Lord sent an angel to open the doors and bring out his people. The Lord showed that his power was greater than prison walls.

The Lord is stronger, too, than any walls that threaten to bind you. If you feel hemmed in by a prison of your circumstances, look up to him, the Great Deliverer. Look for the angel or the way he will present for your release.

He will come to you in the nighttime or in the daytime of your grief. He will send his angels to surround you and bring you out.

Prayer focus for today: Those who are addicted to alcohol.

As God has said: "I will live with them and walk among them, and I will be their God, and they will be my people." (2 Corinthians 6:16)

The incarnation of Jesus Christ has been described as "God putting skin on." What an overwhelming miracle that was. Think of it! The God of the universe, who created heavens, earth, and universe, cared so much for mere mortals that he was willing to become one of us. He left his rightful place in Glory to be born of a virgin, live a sinless life, and die on a cross to save our souls.

Our God said he'd live with us. He told us he'd walk among us. And he did by putting skin on! What should our response be to this awesome truth?

Our response should be one of profound gratitude. He is our God. We are his people. He knows from skin experience how we feel. He understands our bereavement. He walked the same path we are walking today. For this we should bow down before him and bless his holy name.

Prayer focus for today: Migrant farmworkers.

DECEMBER 25

"Glory to God in the highest, and on earth peace to men on whom his favor rests." (Luke 2:14)

We see bumper stickers promoting peace. Mass media gurus tout the peace efforts of world leaders. We pray for peace in our churches.

There's nothing wrong with desiring peace. But seeking peace for its own sake is a lot like tilting at windmills. It's putting all the emphasis on the product without considering the process that is necessary to produce the product.

The only true peace comes when glory is given to God. When people get their priorities straight and give God the glory in all things, peace abounds.

So it can be with you, dear child of God. You may long for peace in your soul now in this time of bereavement. Your insides are in turmoil. You may feel totally restless.

What is the solution? Give glory to God who is in the highest. Then peace will embrace and cover you.

Prayer focus for today: Blessings on those who celebrate Christmas as Christ's birthday.

You know when I sit and when I rise; you perceive my thoughts from afar. (Psalm 139:2)

If you've ever been in charge of a group of children, you know what a challenge it is to keep track of them all. They go here and there, up and down. It's a little like trying to keep a bunch of corks submerged in water!

Try to imagine, then, what it must be like for our God, our Abba Father, as he keeps track of each of his children. He knows when each of us sits, stands, runs, or walks. Certainly at times, we act like a bunch of corks in water.

He not only sees all our actions, but he also knows all our thoughts. He knows our frustrations and our anger. He knows our fears when we're left alone and he knows when we feel like quitting. He knows it all!

The wonder of all this is that he is a God who sees and cares deeply for each of us. The miracle of all this is that he loves us no matter what we do or think. He knows us better than we know ourselves.

He's waiting to be our Abba Father.

Prayer focus for today: Missing children.

DECEMBER 27

"Man born of woman is of few days and full of trouble. He springs up like a flower and withers away; like a fleeting shadow, he does not endure." (Job 14:1–2)

The Scriptures tell us that in the scheme of eternity, our lives are only a few days. Whether those few days are twenty, fifty, or seventy years, we are told we will not endure in this flesh.

We cannot choose our number of days for ourselves or for others. When my husband died, we were all numb from the suddenness. One of our Christian friends sat in my dining room, shook his head and said, "The Lord didn't consult me on this. I could have suggested some other people!" This dear friend was grieving in his own way.

A little later, the group who thronged to my house right after my husband's death began a praise service. We sang. We worshipped. We praised God for the resurrection he promised us. The reality of a life withered away was covered in the sheer joy of knowing that a soul had gone to be with his Lord.

Today may you experience joy such as this!

Prayer focus for today: Children whose fathers deserted the family.

DECEMBER 28

Prepare your minds for action; be self-controlled.
(1 Peter 1:13)

It's intriguing to watch marathon runners. You can almost feel the intensity of their concentration. As the race goes on, the packs of athletes begin to spread out. The runners establish their pace according to what they can do or according to how well they have prepared.

My daughter-in-law participates in marathons. She didn't just decide one day she'd do it. She planned months ahead. She studied what would be necessary. She engaged a trainer and followed the prescribed routines and suggestions. She learned persistence. She exercised self-control to be able to complete what she set out to do.

In the same way, our Lord asks us to prepare our minds for what we are called to do in our lives. Even when we are in a different marital situation than we planned, we are called to set our minds on what he has called the rest of our lives to be.

Thank you, Lord.

Prayer focus for today: Church youth groups.

DECEMBER 29

Turn to me and be gracious to me, for I am lonely and afflicted. (Psalm 25:16)

One of the most hurtful things that can happen to us is for people to turn their backs on us or to ignore us. It makes us feel we don't count, that we're not accepted.

There is one who never turns his back on us. Praise God! We, in our time of sorrow, may "feel" that he has turned away. We may fret and complain of our affliction. But he is there all the time.

He is waiting with his prevenient grace for us to turn to him. He wishes, then, that we don't turn from him. We are totally accepted by him, the great God of the Universe.

Today, promise yourself, and him, that you will turn to him.

Prayer focus for today: A cure for cancer and for those afflicted.

The LORD upholds all those who fall and lifts up all who are bowed down. (Psalm 145:14)

One of the many modern conveniences is the elevator. Think of it. You enter. The doors close. You are lifted up to a higher level. Those elevators with glass sides give you a special vista of where you've been and where you're going.

Have you ever thought of the word "elevator"? To elevate means to raise or uplift. But, you may ask, "Don't elevators also go down?" The opposite of elevate is degrade or belittle. Wouldn't you rather think of this invention purely as an "elevator" rather than a "degrader"?

Try to think of our Lord as an elevator. He raises us up. He lifts up those who fall. He gently holds out his hands to pull up those who are bowed down. He is a spotless "elevator" and never a degrader.

So today, if you're bowed down with the realities of being thrust into singlehood, look to the one who is eager to elevate you to heights you never before dreamed of.

Hallelujah!

Prayer focus for today: Children who are language delayed.

DECEMBER 31

"Surely I am with you always, to the very end of the age." (Matthew 28:20)

Just before our Lord left this world, he promised what we see in this verse from Matthew. He begins with the adverb "surely," which indicates certainty.

And then he tells us, "I am with you always." Not "I will be," but "I *am* with you." For how long? Always, forever, and with no exceptions.

He didn't say, "I'll be with you as long as you are married," or "As long as you are grateful to me," or "As long as you do what's right." He said, "For always."

No matter how bleak your life may seem to be for now, know that the great "I Am" is with you for all eternity—"to the very end of the age."

Prayer focus for today: Blessings on those who rest on the true hope in Jesus.